ESTATE PLANNING
for the Informed Consumer

A Practical Guide to Protecting Your Assets from Probate, Nursing Home Costs and Taxes

---

Edward D. Beasley, JD, LLM

David H. Ferber, JD

Gregory B. Gagne, ChFC

Cover design, book design and layout by Jim L. Friesen

Library of Congress Control Number: 2017935871

International Standard Book Number: 978-0-9789845-2-6

Printed in the United States of America by Mennonite Press, Inc., Newton, Kansas. www.MennonitePress.com

Published by Beasley & Ferber, PA, Concord New Hampshire, and Affinity Investment Group, LLC, Exeter, New Hampshire.

For additional copies, send $24.95 plus $3.00 shipping and handling per book to:

Beasley & Ferber, PA
55 Hall Street
Concord, NH 03301
(603) 225-5010
www.beasleyferber.com

or

Affinity Investment Group, LLC
18 Hampton Road, Unit 7
Exeter, NH 03833
(603) 778-6436
www.affinityinvestmentgroup.com

Table of Contents

About the Authors

EDWARD D. BEASLEY, JD, LLM, is the founder of Beasley & Ferber, PA, an Estate Planning and Elder Law firm with offices in Concord, Bedford, Nashua and Exeter, New Hampshire and North Andover, Massachusetts. He received his Bachelor's Degree, Summa Cum Laude, Phi Beta Kappa from Dartmouth College (1974), his JD degree, Cum Laude, from Washington & Lee University (1978) and his LLM degree in Taxation from Boston University (1982).

Mr. Beasley has written and published numerous articles on Estate Planning and Elder Law and has appeared as a panelist on many Elder Law and estate planning symposiums. He has appeared as a featured guest on NBC Nightly News in a segment entitled "Inheritance Disputes," and was featured in a USA Today cover story entitled, "Fighting Over the Care of Aging Parents." He is a co-author of the books, *Alzheimer's Disease: Fighting for Financial Survival, The Nursing Home Crunch, Asset Protection and Retirement in New Hampshire, Asset Protection and Retirement in Massachusetts and Trusts for the Average Person: The Optimum Estate Plan.*

Mr. Beasley is a former chair of the Elder Law Committee of the ABA, and is a member of the National Academy of Elder Law Attorneys and of the New Hampshire chapter of the

National Academy of Elder Law Attorneys. He is recognized nationally as an expert in the field of Elder Law, Medicaid, and nursing home planning and asset preservation techniques for those afflicted with mental, physical and developmental disabilities. He is a recipient of Martindale-Hubbell's highest "AV" peer review rating. He is a member of the bars of New Hampshire, Massachusetts, Rhode Island and Virginia.

DAVID H. FERBER, JD, is a partner with Beasley & Ferber, PA. He received his Bachelor's Degree in psychology, Magna Cum Laude, Phi Beta Kappa, from Columbia University (1981) and his JD also from Columbia University (1984), where he was a member of the Columbia Human Rights Law Review.

Mr. Ferber is a nationally published author of articles on estate and Medicaid Planning, including articles on the Deficit Reduction Act, the Joint Revocable Trust as a tool for estate planning, annuities in Medicaid Planning, among others. He is a co-author of the books, *Alzheimer's Disease: Fighting for Financial Survival, The Nursing Home Crunch, Asset Protection and Retirement in New Hampshire, Asset Protection and Retirement in Massachusetts and Trusts for the Average Person: The Optimum Estate Plan.* He is a lecturer on Estate and Medicaid Planning, having given presentation on these topics for other attorneys, social workers /case managers, and the general public. He has been a guest on WMUR-TV and WGIR-Radio, speaking about nursing home planning.

Mr. Ferber is a former Vice Chair and Newsletter Editor of the Elder Law Committee of the American Bar Association and is a member of the National Academy of Elder Law Attorneys and of the New Hampshire and Massachusetts chapters of the National Academy of Elder Law Attorneys. He is a member of the bars of New Hampshire, Maine and Massachusetts and a former member of the bar of Connecticut.

GREGORY B. GAGNE, CHFC, is the founder of Affinity Investment Group, LLC, an investment advisory firm registered with the US Securities and Exchange Commission. His firm offers wealth management and distribution planning services for retirees or those planning to retire.

After earning his Bachelor of Science, a dual degree in economics and finance from Bentley College in 1991, Mr. Gagne became a Chartered Financial Consultant in 2001, following completion of courses in estate planning, financial planning, business planning, income tax and retirement and pension planning through the American College.

Mr. Gagne is past president of the New Hampshire Association of Insurance and Financial Advisors, having served previously in many chairs of its local board. He serves on several boards of directors and believes strongly about giving back to the community.

Mr. Gagne has garnered national exposure in professional trade magazine articles and is co-author of the books: *Asset Protection and Retirement in New Hampshire*, *Asset Protection and Retirement in Massachusetts* and *Trusts for the Average Person: The Optimum Estate Plan*. He frequently is featured writing on topics such as practice management, planning techniques and goal setting.

Introduction

We wrote our first book, *Alzheimer's Disease: Fighting for Financial Survival*, over 15 years ago. As all of our clients know, the older one gets, the faster time goes. In some ways, it seems like we wrote our first book just yesterday. In other ways, due to the monumental changes in our society, it seems like fifteen years ago was the Stone Age. There has been a recession and financial meltdown that brought us to the brink of depression, followed by spectacular growth in the stock market. The government got into the auto business, then got out of it. The price of gasoline rose to its highest level ever, and then went into free-fall, and we had a presidential election like none in our nation's history. The winter of 2014-2015 had record snowfall and blizzards, just to be followed by one of the mildest winters ever. Since publication of our first book, our society has experienced massive social change on an unprecedented scale, and the world of print is rapidly giving way to the Internet age and information overload.

It is now a different world than it was 15 years ago, or even eight years ago when our last book was published, so we thought that it was time to do some updating. In the pages to follow, you will get a refresher on the basic documents of estate planning, such as wills, powers of attorney and medical directives. Though these topics do not change much over time, there have been important updates that you need to know about. Next we will get in to the Medicaid rules and asset preservation techniques. As you can imagine, much has changed in these areas, and we will let you know about the latest laws, trends and techniques to protect your hard-earned money and property. We will talk about the legal issues raised by second marriages, as well as the pitfalls of putting your assets into your children's names. We have a new chapter on "Digital Assets," which is a concept that did not even exist when we published our first book. There are chapters on how to leave assets to children with special needs, and how to shelter money from the Massachusetts Estate Tax. Finally, we will present you with the latest information on basic financial and retirement issues that all retired people need to know.

All of our clients have worked very hard for what they have accumulated. Our mission, as it has been for over 25 years, continues to be to help people preserve their assets from the exorbitant cost of nursing homes, and to help them pass on their lifetime of savings in the easiest, most secure and least expensive way. We hope that you enjoy this book, that you learn a thing or two that will help your family's bottom line, and that you will be motivated to take those steps that are necessary to protect what you have worked a lifetime to earn.

David Ferber

Chapter 1
Basic Estate Planning: Wills

A will is a legal document that states who inherits your assets when you die. Although most people understand this basic concept, many misconceptions abound. Most people believe that what you have said in your will about what happens to your assets takes place automatically, that the person you have named as executor simply implements what the will says, and that the courts and legal system do not get involved. The reality, however, is far different. Except between spouses, where the assets are usually owned jointly, a will is generally going to be subject to legal proceeding in Probate Court.

To demonstrate why trusts, and not wills, are the most important document in transferring assets on death, it is useful to trace the path that a will takes when it goes through probate. When you die, your will is filed with the Probate Court for the county in which you lived, along with a petition for appointment of an executor.[1] The person you name in the

[1]This book is written for readers in New Hampshire and Massachusetts. In New Hampshire, the person in charge of a will is called an Executor, whereas in Massachusetts, this person is called a "Personal Representative." In this section of the book, we will use the generic term, "Executor." However, a Personal Representative and an Executor are essentially the same thing.

will as executor does not automatically become executor on your death. That is, when you name someone in your will to act as executor, it is only a nomination, and not an appointment. Only the Probate Court has legal authority to appoint an executor. The court will almost always follow your nomination, but it is not required to do so.

For example, say you nominate your son as executor. Some years after you have signed your will, your son is convicted of embezzlement, tax evasion or fraud, and goes to prison. You fail to change your will and you pass away with your son still being named as executor. Being an executor is a position of trust and confidence, and involves handling money and property. Therefore, it is unlikely that the court will honor your will and appoint him. Or, say your son dies before you, or becomes seriously ill, or for some other reason is unable to act as executor. In this case, the court has no choice but to name someone else to wrap up your estate.

Another common fallacy is that there is a "reading of the will" by the decedent's attorney. While a reading of the will can make for a dramatic scene in a murder mystery, what happens in real life is far more routine. As mentioned above, the will is filed with the local probate court, at which point it becomes a public document. Any interested party (or anyone, for that matter) may obtain a copy and read it for themselves.

What makes a document a valid will? Even if a document has the word "Will" in the title, it does not automatically qualify to be valid. If you type your final wishes on your computer, if you scribble them on a hospital menu as you near death, or if you jot them down on the proverbial cocktail napkin, you have not created a will. To be valid, a will must be prepared strictly in accordance with certain formalities required by law.

Many a document that everyone thought was a will has not been honored by the courts because it failed to be signed with the proper formalities.

First and foremost, the will needs to have been signed by the decedent (known as the "testator") in the presence of two witnesses. All three people (testator and witnesses) need to have signed in the presence of each other and in the presence of a notary public. Any adult who is mentally competent can be a witness. However, if one of the witnesses to a will is also a beneficiary of that will, then the gift to that person is void unless two other disinterested witnesses sign the will. To be safe, the witnesses should be completely independent people. They should not be family members or beneficiaries of the will. After the testator and witnesses have signed, a notary needs to sign a formal affidavit attesting to the manner of execution. If such an affidavit, known as a "self-proving affidavit," has not been signed, then one of the witnesses will need to testify in court as to the manner of execution of the will. To some extent, this requirement has been relaxed in New Hampshire. A 2014 law says that if a will is not contested, the court may approve it with the written agreement of the surviving spouse, beneficiaries, next of kin (*i.e.*, legal heirs), or if there are charitable beneficiaries, the relevant official of the Attorney General's office.

Most wills state that the executor is to serve without bond, or with a minimum bond. In this respect, the practice is dramatically different in New Hampshire and Massachusetts. A probate bond is a type of insurance contract. In exchange for payment of a premium, the insurance company will make good on any losses caused by the executor's dishonesty or theft of funds. In New Hampshire, even if the will directs the executor serve without posting a bond, the Probate Court will order that one be purchased. In Massachusetts, the Probate Court will also require that the executor post a bond. However, if the parties who are interested to the will agree, the court will often not require that the bond be purchased through an insurance company.

The amount of the bond will be set proportionately to the size of the estate, *i.e.*, the larger the estate, the larger the bond. Once the bond has been set, though, the court will typically allow the amount of the bond to be lowered, if all of the interested parties consent. This can be important, since the higher the amount of the bond, the more it costs. The bond premium is paid annually, and the bond must be renewed if the probate proceeding lasts more than one year. Although the New Hampshire Probate Courts typically give the executor thirty days to purchase the bond, it is not unusual for the bonding process to take a good deal longer. Typically, the larger the amount of the bond, the longer the insurance company takes to complete the paperwork. Therefore, it is not unusual for the executor to have to ask the Probate Court for an extension of time to obtain the bond.

In recent years, bonding companies have become more and more strict in their standards as to whom they will insure, and getting a probate bond is not always easy. This is especially true in large estates. Sometimes, people file probate petitions "pro se," *i.e.*, on their own, without a lawyer. Purchasing a bond in these cases can be difficult, since sometimes bonding companies do not like to issue bonds without attorneys involved. Furthermore, if the executor has filed bankruptcy in the past, or if he or she has credit problems, it is not unusual for the bonding company to refuse to issue the bond. Not only can this cause the executor embarrassment and loss of privacy (the executor has to explain to the family as to why he cannot be bonded), but it leads to delays and extra expense. In such a case, someone else needs to petition the court to become executor, and the whole process begins again. In the meantime, the decedent's bills are not getting paid and the assets are not being managed. Credit card companies, car loan companies and mortgage companies are not, on the whole, sympathetic to the explanation that their bills are not being paid due to delays in getting an executor appointed.

After the will has been accepted by the court and the bond has been obtained, then the court formally appoints the executor by issuing a "Certificate of Appointment." This an official document with the court seal, and gives the executor legal authority to act. One of the first duties of the executor is to notify the parties who have a legal interest in the estate. New Hampshire and Massachusetts have somewhat different requirements in this regard, but, in essence, the idea is that anyone who is involved in the will or the estate has a right to be informed about the proceedings and to know who has been appointed executor. Within three months of appointment, the executor makes an inventory of all of the assets to be probated, and reports that inventory, under oath to the court. The inventory stays on file with the court and is a matter of public record.

Creditors who have any claims against the estate present them to the executor. Some years ago, the US Supreme Court held that if an executor has knowledge of a creditor (a credit card, for example) then he or she is required to notify the creditor that an estate has been opened. If the claim is valid, then the executor must pay it out of the decedent's assets. If the executor disputes the claim, then he or she notifies the creditor that the claim is being denied. It is then up to the creditor to decide whether to bring suit to enforce the claim. Of course, if the executor and creditor agree, the claim may settled. If there are any taxes due to the state or the IRS, the executor needs to obtain a release from the relevant taxing authority, *i.e.*, a document stating that all taxes are paid.

One problem that has tended to crop up in recent years concerns collection agencies. Sometimes the family may not have known about a small credit card or medical bill. If the bill remains unpaid for some time, the creditor frequently turns it over to a collection agency. The collection agency files a claim with the Probate Court, sends a copy to the executor, and the executor pays the bill. This sounds simple, but look at what usually happens next. The Probate Court will not allow the estate to be closed unless all bills are paid, and will require the executor to obtain a release of the claim from the collection agency. The problem here is that once the bill is paid, collection agencies lose all interest and, in the authors' experience, will not be cooperative. They do not return phone calls or answer letters, and dealing with them can be an exercise in frustration. The executor is then forced to report this to the Probate Court and file a motion asking the court to allow the filing of a cancelled check as proof of payment. The court will agree, but filing the motion, and waiting for the court to respond only adds to the expense and delay of the probate proceeding.

At the end of the probate proceedings, the executor makes a report to the court of all that he or she has done, as well as a report of the income and expenses of the estate. This report is known as an "accounting." It is only after the judge approves of the accounting that the assets can be distributed to the beneficiaries. The procedures for approval of an accounting are somewhat different in New Hampshire and Massachusetts, with New Hampshire's being stricter.

In Massachusetts, if the assets to be probated do not exceed $25,000 plus a car, then full-fledged probate is not required. Rather, a simplified procedure known as "Voluntary Administration" is used. With Voluntary Administration, there are many fewer formalities and requirements than under regular probate administration. New Hampshire used to have a Voluntary Administration procedure, but the legislature abolished it a few years ago. Now, all estates in New Hampshire, regardless of size, are subject to the same basic probate process. However, New Hampshire has enacted two procedures to simplify probate in certain cases. Where the sole beneficiary of the will is a spouse, only child or a trust and if the spouse or child is also nominated as executor, he or she may take advantage of "Waiver of Administration." Here, the court appoints the person as executor and then has very little further involvement. In other cases, assuming that all debts and taxes have been paid and there are no objections or complications, then the executor may elect to use a procedure known as "Summary Administration." In Summary Administration, if the rquirements have been met and if six (6) months have passed since appointment of the executor, then the estate may be closed without the necessity of filing an account.

In 2012, Massachusetts adopted a law known as the Massachusetts Uniform Probate Code (MUPC). The MUPC is long and complex and an explanation of it is way beyond the scope of this book. (The Massachusetts court system has published a manual as to how to comply with the MUPC.

To illustrate how complex the law is, the manual is about 170 pages long.) Basically, the MUPC has divided probate cases into different categories, formal vs. informal, and those requiring minimal court involvement vs. those that require a higher degree of court supervision. The MUPC has certainly modernized and clarified probate law, and to this extent the state legislature and the Massachusetts Probate Courts are to be applauded. That being said, the process is still somewhat complex and very slow. Depending on the county the case is filed in, it often takes the court months to act. Probate in Massachusetts is expensive. In all but Voluntary Administration, the filing fee alone is currently $390.

Generally speaking, the advantage of probate is that the court makes sure that the executor does what he or she is supposed to do. If not, the court can remove the executor and, in the worst case, if the executor has misappropriated funds, the bonding company is supposed to pay. There are significant disadvantages of probate: publicity, delay and expense. Probate is a public process. Once your will has been filed with the Probate Court, it is a public document, as is the probate inventory. Thus, who is inheriting your assets, and what and how much they are inheriting from your probate estate is a matter of public record. In these days of widespread fraud and identity theft, making this financial information public can be unwise and even dangerous. Also, wills are fairly easy to challenge. All legal heirs get notice of the estate and appointment of the executor, even people you wanted to disinherit. Since these persons get notice of the will, there can be hard feelings or even a challenge to the will. Even if none of this occurs, you might want to keep your estate more private.

The second disadvantage of probate is the time involved. It is not unusual for Massachusetts Probate Courts to take five or six months to process a probate account. In New Hampshire, even with the Summary Administration process described above, it can easily take nine to twelve months from opening the case until the court closes the estate.

The final disadvantage of probate is the cost. Even with Summary Administration in New Hampshire and the MUPC in Massachusetts, probate is complex and is subject to technical rules and time deadlines. The family has enough to go through when a loved one has died and adding yet another layer of complexity to the mix can make an already difficult situation much worse. Therefore, in all but the simplest of cases, hiring an experienced attorney to handle the probate is a good idea. However, as we all know, attorneys can be expensive. Add to this the cost of the bond (in New Hampshire) and the high court fees (in Massachusetts) probate can be quite a costly undertaking.

The Revocable Trust as a Will Substitute

For the reasons explained above, it is obvious why people would want to spare their families from the delays, cost and publicity of probate. People who wish to avoid probate for their families can take advantage of a trust. A key part of an estate plan which avoids probate is a Revocable Trust, also known as a Living Trust.

A trust is a substitute for a traditional will. A trust says essentially the same thing as a will, *i.e.*, who is going to inherit the assets and who will serve as trustee (the functional equivalent of an executor). The crucial difference between a trust and a will, however, is that a trust is not subject to probate.

You act as sole trustee and manage the trust, using the trust income and principal for whatever you want, without any restriction. Upon your death, the trust continues, with your designated successor trustee (usually your spouse or one of your children), who wraps up the trust in accordance with your wishes. For this reason, the trust avoids the delay, publicity and expense that are involved in probate. A trust is administered privately. Unlike probate, which is published in the newspaper, in which all parties receive notice, and is open to the public, a trust is not. You, as creator of the trust, control who is notified of the trust after your death. The general public has no access to it and neither do any heirs or other persons whom you do not wish to be notified. Second, a trust can be settled quickly. Since a trust does not go to probate, the probate time frames do not apply. In most cases, a trust can be settled in a few weeks.

Consider a hypothetical example of two people, John and Henry, who happen to die on the same day. John had his assets in a trust, and Henry had a will. It would not be unusual for John's trust to be completely settled and the money distributed even before the court has appointed the executor of Henry's will. Therefore, where Henry's beneficiaries are just getting started, John's beneficiaries have already received their inheritance.

Finally, since a trust avoids probate, the trustee usually does not have to hire an attorney. Thus, a trust can be settled with far less expense than a will, since there is no need to pay any attorney's fees after death. Years ago, it was mainly the wealthy who did trusts, while most other people did wills. These days, living trusts have become standard estate planning tools for people of moderate means as well.

The Revocable Trust – Minimizing Massachusetts Estate Taxes for Married Couples

Most of our clients are people of moderate means who are not affected by Federal Estate Taxes. Rather, their primary concerns are avoiding probate and protecting their lifetime of savings from loss to a nursing home. For this reason, we are not going to spend much time on sophisticated tax-saving measures used by the wealthy.

However, there is an important exception for people living in Massachusetts. Massachusetts has a tax known as the "Estate Tax," which applies to all estates valued at $1 million or more. For estate tax purposes, the value of all of the assets, including IRAs, life insurance, stocks, savings and the like, as well as the value of real estate (even non-Massachusetts real estate) is included. With real estate values in Massachusetts at an all-time high, reaching the $1 million mark is not as hard as it may seem.

If a married couple has assets of over $1 million, they can, through the use of two trusts, pass on to their heirs double the exemption amount. Let's look at a married couple whom we will call Harvey and Sheila. On Harvey's death, Sheila takes over as trustee of Harvey's trust and can distribute funds to herself. In addition, a provision is usually inserted in the trust so that she can distribute principal to the children for their health, maintenance, education and support. Using such a two-trust plan can double the Massachusetts estate tax exemption, and can save tens of thousands of dollars from taxes.

Special Nursing Home Issues

Whether you opt for a will or a living trust in your estate plan, you must be very careful if your spouse is ill or needs nursing home care. Naturally, most wills and trusts for married couples leave all of the assets to the surviving spouse. However, if your spouse is a permanent resident of a nursing home you may want to think twice about automatically naming that spouse as beneficiary. The same holds true of your life insurance and IRAs.

Let's say that your spouse is in the nursing home and is receiving Medicaid benefits. Your estate plan is set up so that your will or trust and your life insurance and IRA goes to your spouse. If you die first, and these assets go to your spouse, he or she will immediately lose Medicaid coverage and will have to spend down the inheritance. It is likely that the children will receive nothing.

To avoid this situation, you could have amended your will or trust to say that if you die first, your assets would pass to your children instead of your ill spouse. Of course, you are free to leave your assets to your spouse if you want to; but in our experience most people would rather have the inheritance go to the children, instead of to the nursing home. This is a very simple way of protecting assets from loss to a nursing home. It is very surprising how many people do not even think of it.

Chapter 2
Durable Financial Power of Attorney

Another document that is part of a solid estate plan is a Durable Financial Power of Attorney. Consider this common situation: Lila and Edward have been married for 45 years. For most of their lives, Edward was the primary breadwinner, and by the time he retired, his 401k was worth $450,000. When Lila and Edward were busy working and raising their children, they did not pay much attention to estate planning and after they retired, they were too busy traveling, playing golf and spoiling the grandchildren to attend to business.

One day, Edward had a stroke which left him unable to manage his affairs. In order to obtain funds, Lila needed to access Edward's 401k, but she had never really paid attention to it, and did not know much about it. However, she found the papers and called the brokerage house which managed the funds. She told the representative that she was Edward's wife, and that she needed to take some money from the account to pay bills. The person that she spoke to gave her the bad news. He was unable to help her, since the money belonged to Edward. Not only did Lila not have any authority to have access to the funds, but she was not even entitled to any information about the account. Lila was told the same thing when she called up the company which held Edward's life insurance and stock account. Lila had been stymied because she and Edward never signed durable powers of attorney.

The story gets even worse. Edward's condition declines and he needs nursing home care. As we will see in a later chapter, Lila can protect just about all of the money if she puts it into the proper type of immediate annuity for her benefit. Not having a power of attorney, however, she runs up against the same brick wall. Without the proper legal documentation, she is stuck. She will have to petition the probate court for guardianship, which can be a drawn out, expensive and emotionally painful process.

As we have seen with this example of Edward, (which unfortunately is quite common) someone who has become incompetent does not have the legal capacity to transact business, such as paying bills, signing tax returns, buying or selling property or depositing or withdrawing money from the bank. When an incompetent person has not signed a durable power of attorney, someone such as a spouse, adult child or other interested party must petition the probate court for legal authority to act on the person's behalf. The procedure for obtaining guardianship is similar in New Hampshire and Massachusetts, though there are differences. In New Hampshire, the probate court will hold a hearing and you have to prove to the court's satisfaction that the person over whom you are seeking guardianship (known as a "Ward") cannot take care of his or her financial or business affairs. All of the evidence of incapacity you present needs to be within the past six months, and at least one example needs to be within the past 20 days. The Ward has a right to an attorney, and, if he or she cannot afford an attorney, one will be provided by the state. The Ward can contradict your evidence and present contrary evidence of his or her own. If you believe that it would be harmful for the Ward to attend the hearing or if the Ward is unable to understand what the hearing is about, then you need to ask the court to excuse the Ward's attendance. This will require you to file an affidavit to that effect from the Ward's physician. If the court approves of the guardianship petition, then the court will carefully limit your authority to only those powers that are needed and no more. Where the guardianship concerns money or property (Guardianship over the Estate), the court will order that the guardian post a bond, file an inventory under oath, and make an annual financial accounting. Where the guardianship concerns medical decision making (Guardianship over the Person), then the guardian is required to make an annual report to the court as to the Ward's health, condition and living arrangements.

The process in Massachusetts is similar, though it is called a conservatorship instead of a guardianship and the Ward is called a "Protected Person." In order to obtain a conservatorship, the petitioner files a Medical Certificate with the court. The Medical Certificate must be signed by a licensed medical professional who has evaluated the proposed Protected Person within the past thirty days. The petitioner also files a bond. Notice is given to all interested persons and a hearing is held. At the hearing, the petitioner must furnish an updated Medical Certificate. The Medical Certificate must support the need for the conservatorship. If all of the criteria have been met, then the court appoints the conservator. The conservator collects and holds the Protected Person's assets and pays his or her bills. The conservator is required to file an Inventory with the court within 90 days of the court appointment as well as a financial plan.

The benefits of guardianship/conservatorship are that the court oversees what the guardian/conservator does, and that the guardian/conservator must be bonded. On the other hand, there are significant drawbacks. The proceedings can be time consuming, expensive, cumbersome and emotionally painful for the family. Expenses include attorney's and accounting fees and the annual cost of the bond. There is an emotional cost as well. You need to bring an adversarial court proceeding against a close family member, and have attorneys and the legal system get involved with your family's private affairs. Guardianships and conservatorships are cumbersome. You need to obtain court permission to sell any assets and to do estate planning for the Ward or the protected person. If the Ward or the protected person goes into a nursing home and you want to shelter assets, you will face significant obstacles. Obviously, every case is different, but in general, the authors believe that most people would be better off to structure their affairs to avoid such court proceedings. This can be done by signing a Durable Power of Attorney.

Durable Power of Attorney

A solid estate plan will avoid such court proceedings by including a document known as a "Durable Power of Attorney" (DPOA). If you become incompetent, the holder of your DPOA (called the "Attorney-in-Fact" or "Agent") can transact your business for you, much as a guardian/conservator would do, but without reporting to the probate court or going through any of the probate formalities.[1] Thus, the court hear-

---

[1] For the rest of this chapter, the "Attorney in Fact" will be referred to by the simpler term of "Agent".

ing, Medical Certificate (in Massachusetts), attorneys, bond and accounting fees are all avoided. The family's financial affairs are kept within the family without any involvement by the legal system. If you insert Medicaid Planning provisions in the DPOA, (discussed in later chapters) then the Agent would be able to act to shelter assets should you need nursing home care.

The durable power of attorney document is similar in New Hampshire and Massachusetts. The document contains an itemized list of things that the Agent is able to do, such as:

1. Engage in banking transactions;
2. Collect debts and pay bills;
3. Buy and sell real estate and personal property;
4. Use funds for health, welfare and support;
5. Register and title motor vehicles;
6. Rent a new safe deposit box or enter an existing one;
7. Employ agents, accountants, attorneys or other professionals;
8. Make gifts, if doing so would be beneficial; and/or
9. Deal with IRAs and similar retirement plans.

In fact, a power of attorney can be as formal or informal as desired and can be customized to meet the situation. Usually, each spouse names the other as Agent, with one of the children as a backup. Widowed, divorced or single people typically name one of the children or another trusted person as Agent, with a second child as a backup. The power of attorney can be effective immediately, or it can become effective upon a doctor's certification that you have become unable to manage your financial affairs. However you structure it, though, the key is that the durable power of attorney allows a trusted person to manage your finances without court involvement.

Although powers of attorney are very similar in New Hampshire and Massachusetts, there is one important difference. In New Hampshire, each power of attorney must contain two disclosure statements, one signed by you and the other signed by the Agent. Your statement is a reminder that the Agent has broad powers and essentially is a warning that you need to have the utmost faith and confidence in the Agent. The Agent needs to sign a statement which explains that he or she owes you the highest duties of care, faith and loyalty, and that he or she must at all times act in your best interests.

In either state, you can revoke a power of attorney at any time as long as you are competent. (A power of attorney automatically ends at death.) Likewise, in either state, you can empower your Agent to try to shelter your assets in the event you need nursing home care. The ability to do this is one very distinct advantage of a power of attorney over guardianship or conservatorship. The guardian or conservator can engage in Medicaid Planning with permission of the court; however, this is a cumbersome process and there is no guarantee that the court will approve.

Those with IRAs, 401ks or similar accounts have a particular need for a power of attorney. Recall the case of Edward and Lila with whom we visited at the beginning of this chapter. Edward had become incapacitated, and Lila needed to have access to his IRA. In recent years, IRA and 401k custodians have become increasingly strict in requiring specific language in the power of attorney document that authorizes the Agent to deal with retirement accounts. Since these firms only started to impose this requirement fairly recently, *anyone who has such retirement accounts, and who has a power of attorney that is more than four or five years old, should consider having it re-done to include the required language.*

The Durable Power of Attorney and the Fiduciary Liability Law in New Hampshire

In July 2013, the State of New Hampshire enacted RSA 151-E:19. In part, the law says:

> A fiduciary who possesses or controls the income or assets of a ... [nursing home] resident and has the authority and duty to file an application for Medicaid on behalf of a resident shall be liable ... to the long-term care facility for all costs of care which are not covered by Medicaid due to the fiduciary's negligence in failing to promptly and fully complete and pursue... [a Medicaid application].

For purposes of the law, a "fiduciary" is the holder of your power of attorney or your trustee. The fiduciary is almost always one of your children. Say you go into a nursing home and spend down your assets. For whatever reason, your fiduciary (*i.e*, your child) either files the Medicaid application late or files it but does not properly follow up on it, and as a result your Medicaid benefits are delayed. In this case, your child can be *personally liable* to the nursing home for the cost of your care, at the facility's Medicaid rate until benefits are approved. It goes without saying that this liability can be financially devastating.

Reading between the lines, we see that this law is actually worse than it seems, because the word "negligence" is so vague. As we will see in later chapters, successfully doing a Medicaid application is extremely difficult. For someone who has never done a Medicaid application and who has no experience in knowing what information the state wants or how it should be presented, getting an application through successfully the first time around is close to impossible. Say your Agent files the application, and is diligent about pursuing it, but through no fault of his or her own, it is denied. Is he or she deemed automatically negligent, and therefore liable under the new law? No one really knows because the law does not define what negligence means. Nevertheless, the nursing home has the right to bring a lawsuit alleging negligence in such a case. Even if the lawsuit is not successful, defending against it will be an expensive, time consuming and altogether miserable experience for your Agent. Imagine the devastating effect that this law can have on you and your family.

In order to protect your Agent from a lawsuit under this new law, we very strongly recommend that powers of attorney be written as follows:

A. Your Agent's authority should only become effective when your doctor certifies in writing that you have become incompetent or when you certify in writing that you want such authority to become effective. In this way, your Agent will have notice that his or her authority has started, and will know to be extra careful in monitoring your financial status and if necessary, filing a Medicaid application.

B. The power of attorney should contain a statement to be signed by your Agent that he or she is aware of the Fiduciary Liability Law, that it is especially important to file a Medicaid application on time and that he or she get professional legal help in filing.

C. Finally, your Agent should not sign the disclosure statement, referred to previously. Recall that without the disclosure statement, the power of attorney is not effective. It is the practice of our firm to keep the original durable power of attorney, without the signed disclosure statement, in our safe. Here is the reason: if the Agent has not signed the disclosure statement in advance, then the Agent must meet personally with us so we can prepare it. And when the Agent meets with us, we can advise the Agent of how to do the Medicaid application properly or we can prepare the Application and this way protect him or her from being sued. In our opinion, this procedure is crucial to protect your children from being sued pursuant to the Fiduciary Liability law.

The Fiduciary Liability Law is so important and can have such devastating consequences to the Agent, that we recommend that any durable power of attorney prepared before enactment of the law in July 2013 be revoked and redone with the protective language described above.

Chapter 3
Advance Directives: Living Wills and Medical Powers of Attorney

Let's return to our friends Edward and Lila. When Edward had his stroke, he was taken by ambulance to the emergency room. Lila was not home at the time and when she found out what had happened, she rushed to the hospital. She asked the doctors what had happened and how Edward was doing, but the doctors did not give her any information. Stunned, shocked and in tears, Lila protested that she was Edward's wife, but the doctors were unrelenting. She did not know what to do or where to turn, and she feared the worst. Fortunately, Edward regained consciousness, and gave the doctors permission to speak to Lila.

What happened here? A federal law known as The Health Insurance Portability and Accountability Act of 1996 (HIPAA) prevented Edward's doctors from talking to Lila. In our experience, the HIPAA law has caused families a great deal of trouble and frustration, since doctors are not supposed to release medical information to spouses or adult children. We have even seen cases in which doctors' offices would not let one spouse make medical appointments for another spouse.

No one will dispute that protecting medical information is an admirable goal, but it seems that this law has gone too far.

In any event, if Edward and Lila had prepared a complete estate plan, they would have avoided this problem. Such a plan will include documents known as Advance Directives. In New Hampshire, Advance Directives include a Health Care Power of Attorney and a Living Will. In Massachusetts, the relevant document is called a Health Care Proxy. The Medical Power of Attorney or Health Care Proxy, as the case may be, allows your spouse, adult child or other trusted person you specify to receive confidential medical information and make medical decisions for you if you are unable to do so. If you become incompetent and do not have such a document, your family would need to seek a court guardianship or conservatorship and, until it is approved, they will not be able to get medical information. Clearly, signing the Medical Power of Attorney will avoid lengthy and potentially costly court proceedings in a time of crisis. Medical Powers of Attorney/Health Care Proxies are standard forms and are available at hospitals and doctor's offices. Of course, any client who puts in place a complete estate plan will have such a document included.

The well-known case of Terri Schiavo concerned an unfortunate young woman who suffered irreversible brain damage and became dependent on a feeding tube. Terri's condition led her to be in a vegetative state and she was in a nursing home for 15 years. In 1998 her husband, Michael Schiavo, who was also her guardian, asked the court for authority to remove her feeding tube. Terri's parents opposed him. Although the lower court found that Terri would not wish to continue life-prolonging measures, the court appeals lasted for seven years. There was international news coverage and even Congress got involved. Ultimately, in March 2005, the feeding tube was removed and she died at age 41.

The seven-year court battle and the turmoil that Terri's family was forced to endure were completely preventable. The basic problem was that Terri did not execute an Advance Directive during her life. Because there was no written documentation, Terri's husband was able to argue to the courts that Terri would not have wanted heroic measures to prolong a certain death. Terri's parents were able to argue the opposite. The truth about Terri's opinion, if indeed she even had an opinion, could not be known.

This case was tragic. Terri was stricken at a young age and languished in a nursing home for the next 15 years. In addition, her family was torn apart and had to spend fortunes on pointless legal battles. The further tragedy is that it was all preventable. Had Terri only executed an Advance Directive, her wishes would have been known and the medical system would have been legally bound to carry out those wishes. Whether or not you believe in heroic end-of-life matters is intensely personal. There is no right or wrong answer. What is definitely wrong though, is to leave your loved ones in the dark about your wishes.

Chapter 4
The Medicaid Rules

These days, a long-term nursing home stay can spell financial disaster for most people. The annual cost of a typical nursing home is between $110,000 and $120,000. Very few people can withstand these costs before being financially wiped out. Although there are some "protections" for married couples, they are meager and can easily lead to a life of poverty or near poverty for the spouse at home. Let's start at the beginning, though, and explain how nursing homes are financed.

A. The Difference Between Medicare and Medicaid

Medicare is the basic health insurance program available to anyone who is disabled or over 65 and who has paid into the Social Security system. Many people believe that Medicare pays for long-term nursing home care. However, people who believe this and who later enter a nursing home are in for a very unpleasant and expensive surprise, since Medicare is *not* designed to cover long-term nursing home care. If a Medicare beneficiary is admitted to a hospital for three nights and then goes to a nursing home for rehabilitation, Medicare will pay the nursing home in full for the first 20 days, and in part from day 21 to 100.[1] However, once the patient stops making improvement, Medicare and any Medicare supplement insurance stop paying, even if this occurs before expiration of the hundred days. Medicare for skilled nursing care is meant to be a short-term benefit only. People who need long-term nursing home care are not covered.

B. Three Ways of Paying for Nursing Homes

Since Medicare will not cover long-term care, what will? There are three ways to pay for a nursing home stay: long-term care insurance, private payment, and Medicaid.

1. Long-Term Care Insurance

Long-term care insurance is a type of health insurance that will pay for prolonged nursing home stays, provided that the conditions of the insurance policy are met. Depending on the policy, payment can be for as little as two years or for as long as a lifetime. The insurance can pay anywhere from a minimal amount of the nursing home charges all the way to payment in full. The better policies come with an "inflation rider," which means that the policy benefit rises each year. Some policies also include payment for home health care. Since nursing home insurance decreases people's reliance on Medicaid, the government has enacted policies that encourage people to buy this insurance. Under federal law, the premiums for certain long-term care policies are in

---

[1]Beware of going to the hospital and being placed on "observation status." Observation status is a designation used by hospitals to bill Medicare. If you are in the hospital for "observation status," and then go to a nursing home for rehabilitation, Medicare will not pay for your nursing home stay.

part tax deductible as a medical expense. In Massachusetts, if you have a long-term care policy which pays at least $125 per day for two years and if you need Medicaid assistance, the state will not put a lien on your house.

Unfortunately, long-term care insurance is not practical for most people. First, it is too expensive for most retired people to afford. Second, not everyone qualifies for the insurance. That is, you might not meet the health standards the insurance company requires in order to issue a policy.

2. Private Payment

Since relatively few people have long-term care insurance, most people who enter the nursing home begin by paying privately with their own funds. The problem, of course, is that nursing homes are extremely expensive, with costs of $11,000 to $12,000 a month being common. When the money runs out, nursing home residents are forced to turn to the next method of payment which is Medicaid.

3. Medicaid

Medicaid is a federal program that is administered by the states. It pays for medical treatment and room and board at the nursing home when you have run out of funds. In Massachusetts, Medicaid is also known as Mass Health. For the remainder of this book, the term "Medicaid" will refer both to the New Hampshire and Massachusetts version of the program. The Medicaid laws are very similar in both states, and we will point out any differences.

a. Applying for Medicaid

In order to qualify for Medicaid, you must meet certain medical and financial requirements. First, you must either live in a nursing home or have a medical need that requires nursing home care.

In New Hampshire, applications for Medicaid benefits are filed with the Medicaid District Office covering the geographical area in which the applicant lives. In Massachusetts, applications are filed at a central office in Charlestown.

In New Hampshire, after an application is received, the District Office will schedule a personal interview with a case technician. The technician will go over the documentation that was submitted with the application, and will give you a list of any further information that is needed. In Massachusetts, there is no personal interview, and all communication is done by mail. The enrollment center will mail out a document known as an "Information Request." This is a questionnaire calling for you to supply any missing documentation and to explain any documentation about which the case technician has any questions.

In either state, the key to filing a successful Medicaid application is to obtain the proper documentation, which is known as "verifications." At a minimum, you will have to provide the following verifications:

1. Copy of deed or lease, to prove your residence;
2. Copy of birth or baptismal certificate, naturalization certificate, or green card;

3. Social Security, Medicare and private health insurance cards. If there is private health insurance, then a copy of the latest bill will also be required;

4. Marriage certificate, and, for widows or widowers, a marriage certificate plus a death certificate of the spouse;

5. Bank account statements for the past 60 months. You will need to explain and document any large or unusual deposits and withdrawals;

6. Statement of nursing home personal needs account;

7. Life insurance policies and five years' worth of annual statements of the cash value;

8. Copy of durable power of attorney;

9. Copy of trust documents, along with verification of all assets in the trust name;

10. Copy of prepaid burial contract and cemetery deed;

11. Verification of all other financial assets, such as stocks, bonds, mutual funds, etc., and their value, plus sixty months' worth of statements. As with bank accounts, large deposits and withdrawals will need to be explained and verified;

12. Copies of any annuity contracts;

13. Verification of any assets transferred within the past sixty months. This requirement applies not only to gifts, but to any asset sold within the relevant time frame. In the case of a house sale, for example, a closing statement will be required, as well as proof of deposit of the closing proceeds. The spenddown of these proceeds will also have to be accounted for;

14. Verification of all income, such as Social Security award statements and pension check stubs. For

income that is direct deposited, a bank statement will suffice; and/or

15. If bank accounts or other assets have been closed in the past five years, an accounting of the proceeds of these accounts.

Providing these verifications is tedious and is the most difficult part the application process. It is also of the utmost importance. An application will not be approved until all verifications have been provided and all issues raised by the verifications have been explained. The burden of providing the verifications is on the applicant; the Medicaid office will not assist you in getting these documents.

There are strict time deadlines in providing the verifications. An application in which the verifications are not provided within the deadlines will be denied. For this reason, it is advisable to assemble the verifications before filing the application and to make sure that those verifications are complete. For example, most bank statements contain from two to five pages. Often, one or two of these pages do not contain any useful information, but rather contain blank forms so you can balance the account or contain a cover page with the bank's name and latest savings or loan rates. Even though these pages do not contain any useful information, they must be produced.

In New Hampshire, while most of the Medicaid case technicians try to be helpful and understanding, it is important to know that the interview and application process is lengthly and frequently can be grueling. As of this writing, it is not unusual for the State of New

Hampshire to take five to seven months to issue an eligibility decision. Massachusetts typically takes about half of this time.

It is of the utmost importance that the information disclosed on the Medicaid application be accurate and truthful, since any willful misrepresentation can be prosecuted as fraud. If you make a statement on the application that you believe to be accurate, but which later turns out not to be so, you will not be in trouble as long as you promptly report the error. Likewise, if you file the application and later discover that the applicant had assets you did not know about, you will not be in trouble as long as you report it. The key is to promptly report the new facts you have discovered. You are only held to the standard of honesty and good faith, not perfection.

If Medicaid is denied and you believe that the denial was in error, you can request an appeal that is known as a "Fair Hearing." The process of claiming a Fair Hearing is simple and informal. However, there are strict time deadlines for doing so. The Fair Hearing is not a second chance. Rather, it is a proceeding at which you will have to prove that the caseworker wrongfully denied the application due to a mistake of fact or a mistake in applying the law. Fair Hearings are conducted by a "hearings examiner," who is an employee of the Medicaid agency. At a Fair Hearing, each side will have the ability to offer evidence and present the legal and factual basis of his or her case. Although the testimony is taken under oath and witnesses are subject to cross-examination, the proceedings are far less formal than those of a courtroom. Unfortunately, in New Hampshire at least, it can take up to nine months to get a decision from the hearings examiner after the hearing is conducted.

Under federal law, a nursing home cannot discriminate, discharge or in any way alter the treatment of a Medicaid patient. The only difference in treatment between Mediciad patients and private-pay patients is that Medicaid patients cannot have a private room. *Additionally, any facility that accepts Medicare or Medicaid has no legal right to require that other family members contribute to the payment, or guarantee payment. Any contracts providing such guarantees are void.*

b. Medicaid's Financial Requirements
1. General Rules

Medicaid law puts very strict limits on the amount and type of assets that a recipient is allowed to have. For Medicaid purposes, assets are classified as "countable" or "non-countable." There are strict limits on your countable assets and there are no limits on your non-countable assets. The primary non-countable assets are as follows:

1. Your home, provided that your spouse (or certain limited classes of relatives) are living there. Note that only one residence is exempt, so that if you have a vacation home, investment property or second home, the non-homestead property will be countable;
2. Irrevocable prepaid funeral;
3. A $1,500 bank account earmarked for burial expenses;
4. One burial plot;

5. Essential household items, such as appliances, clothing, household furnishings and personal, non-investment jewelry;
6. Property subject to legal proceedings, such as probate;
7. Lump-sum death benefits for funeral and burial expenses;
8. Income tax refunds;
9. One motor vehicle;
10. Cash value of life insurance policies, up to $1,500;
11. Term life insurance, with no cash value; and/or
12. Cash assets up to $2,000 in Massachusetts and $2,500 in New Hampshire.

All other assets are countable. Examples of countable assets are bank accounts, IRAs and similar retirement accounts, cash value of life insurance above $1,500, stocks, bonds and mutual funds, second homes, second cars, deferred annuities, and anything else of whatever kind or description that can be sold or turned into cash. If you have countable assets over the allowable limit, you will not be eligible for Medicaid until you have spent down to the limit. This process is known as the "spenddown," and is discussed later. Alternatively, and the very point of this book, is that *there are certain very powerful Medicaid Planning devices you can use to preserve most, not all, of your countable assets, and still allow you to qualify for Medicaid.*

Medicaid has separate rules for income. In the case of an unmarried person, all of the income, with certain exceptions, must be paid to the nursing home. You are allowed to keep a minimal "personal needs allowance," of approximately $70.00 per month, as well as sufficient money to pay for health insurance premiums. In the case of a married couple, the income of the at-home spouse is not counted, while the income of the institutionalized spouse is counted. The at-home spouse does have the benefit of certain income protections, discussed below.

2. Division of Assets for Married Couples

Under a law ironically known as the "Spousal Impoverishment" provisions of the Medicare Catastrophic Coverage Act of 1988, the at-home spouse benefits from certain minimal asset protections.[2] In our opinion, these protections can hardly be called protections at all. In New Hampshire, the Community Spouse is allowed to keep half of the couple's countable assets, or $120,900, whichever is less. In Massachusetts, the Community Spouse is allowed to keep the first $120,900.

Which spouse's name the assets are held in or which spouse brought the assets to the marriage are irrelevant. Many spouses, especially those involved in second marriages, take false comfort from the fact that they hold their assets in separate names, or from the fact that they have entered into a Premarital Agreement. When a spouse in a second marriage enters a nursing home, the Community Spouse is in for an extremely uncomfortable surprise: whose name the asset is in or whether there is a Premarital Agreement is completely

---

[2]For Medicaid purposes, the at-home spouse is known as the "Community Spouse," and the spouse in the nursing home is known as the "Institutionalized Spouse."

irrelevant. When a couple says, "I do," they are, for Medicaid purposes, consenting to treat their assets as if they were jointly held. In the eyes of the law, the marital unit has one pocketbook.

The "protection" provided by the Spousal Impoverishment law is not automatic — the Community Spouse must request it via a procedure known as a "Resource Assessment." Once the Institutionalized Spouse enters a hospital or nursing facility and is likely to remain there for 30 consecutive days or more, the Community Spouse is entitled to have the Resource Assessment done. The Resource Assessment is essentially a financial "snapshot" of the assets on the date of institutionalization. The documentation required to process a Resource Assessment is the same as that needed for a full Medicaid application.

The procedure for a Resource Assessment is as follows: The value of all countable assets are added and divided by two. In New Hampshire, for couples with assets of up to approximately $48,000, the Community Spouse may keep the first $24,180. For those couples with assets above this level, the Community Spouse in New Hampshire may keep half, up to a cap of $120,900. In Massachusetts, the Community Spouse can keep the first $120,900.

3. Treatment of Income for Married Couples

Once the Institutionalized Spouse has met the asset test for Medicaid eligibility, the state will then look at the married couple's income. Subject to deductions for the personal needs allowance and medical insurance, the income of the Institutionalized Spouse must be paid to the nursing home in full. However, depending on the Community Spouse's income, he or she may be allowed to keep some of the income of the Institutionalized Spouse. Under federal law, each state must establish a "Minimum Monthly Maintenance Needs Allowance." (MMMNA). The MMMNA must be at least 150% of the federal poverty line for a family of two, and it rises each year. Currently, the MMMNA is $2,002.50 per month, and the maximum is $3,022.50 per month.

If the Community Spouse's income is below the MMMNA, he or she will be entitled to an "allowance" from the income of the Institutionalized Spouse. The amount of the allowance is determined by a formula set by the federal government. There are two ways of raising the Community Spouse's monthly income allowance. First, if, after getting an income allowance from the institutionalized spouse, the Community Spouse's income remains below the MMMNA, he or she can ask that the *asset allowance* be raised. The idea is to allow the Community Spouse to keep more assets than would normally be allowed with the hope the interest and dividends generated by those assets will provide extra income. Second, the Community Spouse can seek a court order of support against the Institutionalized Spouse. If the court finds that the Community Spouse is entitled to higher income, then the court order would supercede the amount that the state Medicaid agency determined.

4. The Spenddown

Due to Medicaid's strict asset limits, many people need to spend down their assets in order to qualify for Medicaid benefits. If you need to do this, there are certain spenddown strategies that can help you. As mentioned above, certain assets are not countable for Medicaid purposes. It is perfectly permissible to spend money on non-countable assets, as long as you pay fair value for them. For example, you can buy a prepaid funeral or a car. You can buy furniture or personal items, make home improvements and repairs, pay down bills or loans. Care should be taken, however, not to buy items, such as expensive jewelry, artwork, or a luxury car, as these items may be considered to be investments, which could be countable assets.

Whether assets are spent down by making purchases or by paying the nursing home (obviously the last resort), you should pay attention to possible tax consequences. Many people hold the bulk of their wealth in retirement assets such as IRAs and 401ks. While the income tax treatment of these assets is beyond the scope of this book, there are significant income tax consequences when these assets are liquidated. The same is true of appreciated assets such as stocks and real estate and assets with a taxable component, such as savings bonds and annuities. Since cashing in these assets can lead to income taxes, it is often advisable to consult with an accountant or financial advisor prior to finalizing plans as to the order in which assets should be liquidated.

Spending down in accordance with the state requirements, however, can be viewed as a last resort. We have already seen some modest techniques which can minimize what the institutionalized spouse and community spouse have to spend. The field of Medicaid Planning, which we discuss in later chapters, can actually allow you to save the bulk of your wealth, sometimes all of it, while making you eligible for Medicaid.

Chapter 5
Transfer of Asset Rules and Deficit Reduction Act

In order to have a complete understanding of Medicaid law, you need to know the transfer of asset rules. People applying for Medicaid need to disclose transfers of liquid assets or real estate made within sixty months before the date of application. This sixty-month time period is referred to as the "lookback period." If assets are given away during the lookback period, then Medicaid will assess a penalty: For every $9,963 (in New Hampshire) or $10,767 (in Massachusetts) given away, there will be a period of Medicaid ineligibility of one month. The disqualification period (sometimes called a "penalty period") starts to run from the date when the individual enters a nursing home *and* would otherwise be eligible for Medicaid coverage, *i.e.*, when the person has under $2,500 (in New Hampshire) or $2,000 (in Massachusetts). In other words, the penalty period does not even begin to run until the nursing home resident is out of funds and has applied for Medicaid.

A simple example will show how these rules work. (We will use the New Hampshire figure of $9,963). Let's assume that Uncle Leo gives away $99,630 on January 1, 2017.

At that time, he is perfectly healthy. He suffers a stroke four and one-half years later, and enters the nursing home on June 1, 2021. Let's assume that he has under $2,500 in assets at that time, so he is otherwise eligible for Medicaid. The disqualification as a result of the $99,630 gift that he made four and one-half years ago first starts to run when he applies for Medicaid on June 1, 2021. The disqualification period will run for 10 months from that time, and will end on March 31, 2022. Who will pay for the nursing home during the ten months for which Uncle Leo is disqualified?

The rules as to who pays work very differently in New Hampshire and Massachusetts. In Massachusetts, actually, no one knows who pays. Uncle Leo can't pay, and as a practical matter, the nursing home might have to keep him with only his Social Security and pension, if any, as payment.

In New Hampshire, the situation is more complex. Recall our earlier discussion of RSA 151:E-19 (the Fiduciary Liability law), enacted in July 2013. Another part of this law deals with Medicaid disqualification due to having made gifts. Under the law, if there is a period of Medicaid disqualification due to a gift having been made in the past sixty months, then the recipient of the gift is liable to pay the amount of the gift back to the nursing home. People usually make gifts to their children. By the time the parents need Medicaid later on, the children undoubtedly will have spent the gifted money on tuition, home expenses or other things and will not have the money to return. We have already seen letters from nursing homes to gift recipients threatening to bring suit against them to collect gifted funds. If you ever make gifts to your children (or anyone else), they need to be aware that under this law, they are at risk of being sued by the nursing home for the five-year lookback period following the gift.

There are certain exceptions to the transfer-of-asset rules that pertain to the family home. In these circumstances, a transfer of the home is not penalized:

- To avoid foreclosure;
- To a spouse or to a child who is blind or permanently or totally disabled;
- To an adult child who has lived in the house and provided care to the parent, such that the parent was kept out of the nursing home for two years; and/or
- To a sibling who has an equity interest in the home, and who resided there for at least one year prior to the individual's admission to the nursing home.

The most significant of the above rules is the third one, known as the "Caretaker Child" exception to the transfer-of-asset rules. This law states that if an adult child lives with a parent in the parent's home and provides care to that parent, such that the parent is kept out of a nursing home for two years, then the house may be gifted to the Caretaker Child.

This law is applied differently in New Hampshire and Massachusetts. In New Hampshire, there are no specific rules or regulations governing the standards by which the state analyzes whether the Caretaker Child exception has been met. Usually, an affidavit or letter is submitted from the applicant's doctor or from the child which details the individual's physical condition and need for care, as well as the services provided by the child. The state then determines whether or not it will allow the exception.

In Massachusetts, this rule is interpreted differently. In the case of *Maguire v. Director of the Office of Medicaid* (Mass. Ct.

of Appeals, 2012), Mrs. Maguire's daughter Karen helped her stay at home. Karen testified that she provided her mother with housekeeping services such as cleaning, doing laundry, preparing meals and assisting with medications. However, Mrs. Maguire did not need assistance with the types of activities of daily living, such as dressing, feeding herself, walking, and personal hygiene that would justify her needing nursing home care. Her level of need was such that she could have qualified for assisted living but not a nursing home. Additionally, Karen testified that she was able to leave her mother alone at home for "substantial periods of time" while she was at work. These factors indicated that Mrs. Maguire did not need a nursing home level of care for the two years prior to her move to a nursing home.

When Mrs. Maguire went into a nursing home and applied for Medicaid, the state Medicaid agency denied Karen the benefit of the Caretaker Child exception. When the case went up on appeal, the Court of Appeals said that the evidence indicated that Mrs. Maguire could have been cared for in a community-based setting such as an assisted living facility rather than a nursing home. Therefore, the court upheld the Medicaid agency's denial of the Caretaker Child exception. This decision can be interpreted as stating that those seeking to qualify for the Caretaker Child exception need to prove that they provided a nursing home level of care to the Medicaid applicant. Of course, only a nursing home can provide a nursing home level of care and an adult child who is not a doctor or a nurse really cannot do so. As a result of the *Maguire* case, the standard required in Massachusetts to meet the Caretaker Child exception may, as a practical matter, be impossible to meet.

It remains to be seen how this body of law will develop in Massachusetts.

Theoretically, Medicaid is not supposed to penalize a gift that was made for a purpose other than for Medicaid qualification. An example would be a wedding or graduation gift, or a gift to a grandchild when he or she buys a home. However, proving that a gift was made for a purpose other than for Medicaid eligibility can be an uphill battle. According to the New Hampshire Adult Assistance Manual (the "hands on" manual used by Medicaid caseworkers), a gift is not penalized if:

> The individual provides satisfactory evidence ... that assets were transferred exclusively for a purpose other than to qualify for medical assistance. The individual also provides evidence for the purpose for which the asset was transferred as well as the reason it was necessary to transfer the asset in question for less than fair market value. Assurance that the individual was not considering medical assistance when the asset was disposed of is not sufficient.

Note the language that requires the Medicaid applicant to prove that it was "necessary" to transfer the asset. A gift, by definition, is never "necessary" to make. Further, and, inexplicably as it seems to us, the fact that the Medicaid applicant was healthy and not even thinking of nursing homes when he or she made the gift is irrelevant. For example, if you make a wedding gift to your grandson, you are making it because he is getting married, *not* because you want to protect that money from a nursing home. The state's precluding you from making that explanation, however, seems to defy all logic and common sense. Under these standards, it is questionable whether any gift, however innocent, would ever be allowed.

Under the transfer of asset rules and how they are applied, people of moderate means will be penalized for any gifts they have made during the past five years, regardless of the purpose of the gift. For all practical purposes, the law makes gifting very problematic. Since all gifts are subject to a five-year lookback, someone who makes a gift and then needs nursing home Medicaid assistance within five years can be denied Medicaid benefits, and the people who accepted the gift can be sued.

Chapter 6
Protecting Assets from Devastation Due to Long-Term Care: The Irrevocable Medicaid Trust

As we have seen, the Medicaid rules are harsh, punitive and unforgiving. Any type of planning other than crisis planning must be done at least five years prior to a nursing home stay, which means that pre-planning is more important than ever. A key component of solid estate planning must address how to protect assets from a prolonged nursing home stay. While we endorse and encourage the use of long-term care insurance, we fully realize that most of our clients are, due to health issues, not insurable and many others simply cannot afford the cost of the insurance. As Elder Law Attorneys and estate planners, our clients look to us for legal ways and other financial techniques to protect their assets and solve the issues that confront them now or in the future. We see this as no different from wealthy clients who set up offshore accounts, generation-skipping trusts, or creditor protection trusts. Consequently, for most of our clients, the Irrevocable Medicaid Trust (also known as the "Medicaid Trust") for nursing home protection is a key document in estate planning.

The Medicaid Trust is similar in many ways to the Revocable Trust. You receive all of the income from the trust. The trust can buy and sell assets, including real estate, stocks, bonds, CDs and the like. In fact, this type of trust can own and sell any type of asset or investment other than a tax-deferred retirement account such as an IRA. Upon your death, the trust assets will pass to your heirs without probate, and the trust will terminate. During your lifetime, however, the trust is irrevocable, meaning that you cannot revoke it. The trust is also subject to the five-year Medicaid lookback.

Everyone uses the Medicaid Trust differently. Almost without exception, clients put their house and other real estate (such a cottage on the lake or condo in Florida) into the Medicaid Trust, and leave their liquid assets in the Revocable Trust. Some people put their real estate and a portion of their liquid assets in the Medicaid Trust and the remainder in their Revocable Trust. The point is that the Revocable Trust and Medicaid Trust combination can be tailored to each individual situation.

Even with a Medicaid Trust, you can still change your estate plan if you want to. For example, you can change the trust to leave money to grandchildren who were not even born when the trust was written. Or, say that one of your children is getting divorced and you want to protect the inheritance from his or her ex spouse, or one of your children has developed an alcohol or gambling problem, or one of your children dies before you, leaving children of their own. You can adjust your trust to take account of these changing circumstances. The trust contains a feature known as a "Special Power of Appointment" (SPA). The SPA allows you to change your beneficiaries before death, to take effect when the trust is distributed. Say, for example, the beneficiaries of the trust are your three children, Dick, Jane and Sally, and their children. At any time before your death, you can:

- Adjust how much money Dick, Jane and Sally are getting;
- Disinherit Dick, Jane or Sally, in whole or in part;
- Have the inheritance be held in trust for Dick, Jane or Sally, instead of going to them outright; and/or
- Leave some or all of the inheritance to the children of Dick, Jane or Sally, either outright or in trust for their health, education and support.

Most people use the Medicaid Trust to protect their real estate. Let's take a look in more detail as to how this works. You deed the house into the trust, and then need to wait five years for the protection to accrue. In other words, after five years, if you need nursing home care and apply for Medicaid, the house will not be counted. It will not have to be sold, and it can be passed on to your children. At any time before or after the five-year period, the trust may sell the house and may buy another one. If this is done, the new house will be protected *without* a new waiting period. If the trust sells the house and does not buy another one, then the money received from the house becomes part of the trust *and* will be protected. You will be able to receive the interest and dividends from this money, though the principal will need to remain in the trust until your death. If you put your house into a Medicaid Trust, you do not lose your capital gains advantages. That is, an unmarried person can exempt the first $250,000 from capital gains taxes, and a married couple can exempt the first $500,000, provided they otherwise qualify per the IRS rules. You do not lose these tax advantages if you put your house into the trust. The trust does not file a separate income tax return. The trust assets pass to your heirs with the "stepped-up" tax basis at your death, the same as if the trust did not exist.

There are two drawbacks to putting your house into the Medicaid Trust. First, you may not be able to obtain an equity loan or reverse mortgage on the property. Second, it can become tricky if you have a property tax exemption. If you have a property tax exemption on your house and you put it into the Medicaid Trust, you can maintain the exemption if the trust and/or deed contains a life estate. In New Hampshire, it is often not advisable to retain a life estate, because doing so will allow the state to make a Medicaid Reimbursement Claim against a portion of the house proceeds after your death. Thus, if you have a tax exemption in New Hampshire, these issues need to be addressed carefully. In general, though, the Medicaid Trust is usually an ideal way to protect real estate.

Due to court decisions, the law pertaining to Medicaid Trusts has undergone some changes in recent years. In 2016, the New Hampshire Supreme Court addressed Medicaid Trusts in the case of *Petition of Estate of Thea Braiterman*. The *Braiterman* case is the only New Hampshire Supreme Court case pertaining to Irrevocable Trusts, and therefore it would seem to be an important case. However, the *Braiterman* case is of little practical use to us and our clients, since it is based on an Irrevocable Trust that was written in 1994, and which has long since become obsolete. That is, due to numerous law and policy changes since 1994, our office no longer prepares trusts of the type the Supreme Court addressed in *Braiterman*. Significantly, the *Braiterman* Court said that a properly-written Medicaid Trust would be effective to shelter assets. In the words of the Supreme Court, "Finally, we take this opportunity to stress that we have no doubt that self-settled, irrevocable trusts may, if so structured, so insulate trust assets that those assets will be deemed unavailable to the settlor.... The Trust in this case is not such a vehicle." The conclusion to be drawn from this statement is that a Medicaid Trust which meets today's laws and standards would be effective to shelter assets from long-term care.

In Massachusetts, there has been a more instructive line of cases. Starting in approximately 2011, in response to a 2009 Appellate Court case known as *Doherty v. Director of the Office of Medicaid*, the state started to challenge Medicaid Trusts. Since that time, we have carefully monitored the state's arguments. We have itemized the particular clauses in Medicaid Trusts to which the state has objected. The result of this careful analysis has led us to create a Medicaid Trust which contains none of the language which the state has found offensive. Our current version of the Medicaid Trust contains straightforward and clear language which leaves no doubt whatsoever that only income, and no principal whatsoever, is payable from the trust. In our current version of the trust, there is nothing for the state to attack, and in all of the time that our current trust has been in use, no one, to our knowledge, has ever been denied Medicaid benefits. In other words, the trust successfully shelters assets from long term care.

We are proud to say that our foresight in adapting the Medicaid Trust to meet the state's objections has recently been fully validated. In April 2016, the Massachusetts Appellate Court, in the case of *Heyn v. Office of Director of Medicaid*, reviewed a Medicaid Trust that was, in all material respects, identical to the trusts that our office writes. The *Heyn* Court unequivocally held that an irrevocable Medicaid Trust, if drafted properly, is effective to shelter assets from long-term care costs. Because the trust in the *Heyn* case was virtually indistinguishable from our version of the Medicaid Trust, we can state with confidence that those clients who use it can protect their lifetime of savings, and their home, from depletion to a prolonged nursing home stay.

Chapter 7
Crisis Medicaid Planning

A. Married Couples

In an earlier era, people got married younger than they do today, usually in their twenties. Since most nursing home residents are in their eighties, simple math will tell you that many of them will have been married for fifty or sixty years. In fact, most of these people will hardly ever remember a time in their lives when they were not married. In addition, people of that generation generally have a strong belief in taking care of their family members. It stands to reason that most married people wait until the last possible minute before putting their ill spouse in a nursing home. It is impossible to imagine what goes through the mind of a spouse in this situation. Not only is this person going to live alone for the first time in many decades, but he or she undoubtedly feels tremendous guilt and profound sadness, and feels that they have somehow let down their husband or wife. Almost all of these people have lived very frugal lives, and have deprived themselves and sacrificed in order to put money away. So, when they learn that they are going to have to spend $10,000 to $12,000 dollars a month on the nursing home, and then, due to the harshness of the Medicaid laws, will be forced to live in poverty or near poverty, their feelings of hopelessness and depression must be overwhelming.

While we, as Elder Law Attorneys, cannot remove the emotional devastation of a person who needs to put his or spouse in a nursing home, we can prevent them from suffering financial devastation. Through the creative use of an "Irrevocable, Non-Assignable, Single-Premium Immediate Annuity" (SPIA) it is often possible to shelter 100% of the countable assets from long-term care. This tool can assure that the Community Spouse can continue to lead a life of financial dignity, rather than seeing his or her assets drain away. Fundamentally, an immediate annuity is a very specialized type of contract with an insurance company. The way it works is that the Community Spouse transfers a sum of money to the company in exchange for monthly payments of principal and interest. The length of the repayment term is based on the life expectancy of the Community Spouse.

In the case of a married couple, an SPIA can shelter countable assets, *sometimes as much as 100%*, from long-term nursing home care. This is the result of two different Medicaid laws pertaining to married couples. Recall from our discussion of the spenddown rules that the Community Spouse is allowed to keep a certain amount of money. In New Hampshire, it is half of the monetary assets, up to a cap of $120,900, and in Massachusetts, it is the first $120,900. In New Hampshire, for example, with a married couple having $200,000, the Community Spouse can keep $100,000, and the rest (except for $2,500) would have to be spent down. Significantly (and a huge surprise to many people), the law says that the spenddown funds do not have to be spent on the nursing home! Those funds can be spent for any purpose, as long as fair value is received and as long as they are spent for the benefit of either spouse. The other relevant law concerns *income*. The income of the Community Spouse is completely exempt from the nursing home bills of the Institutionalized Spouse. So, if one spouse is in the nursing home on Medicaid, and the other spouse has a job or otherwise gets income, then such income does not need to be used for the Institutionalized Spouse's nursing home bill.

The key to annuity planning is to re-structure the finances to convert assets, which are fully countable for the nursing home, into income for the Community Spouse, which is exempt. In the above example with a $100,000 spenddown, the Community Spouse uses the spenddown money to buy an immediate annuity and the annuity company makes payments back to the Community Spouse.[1] In this way, the Institutionalized Spouse immediately qualifies for Medicaid, the monthly annuity payments go to Community Spouse, and all of the spenddown money has been protected.

Of course, it is more complex than this. The SPIA needs to comply with three important rules:

1. The length of the repayment term of the annuity can be no longer than the Community Spouse's life expectancy per the relevant government life expectancy tables. For example, let's say Helen, age 80, has a husband in a nursing home. Looking at the relevant life expectancy table, we see that Helen's life expectancy is 9.64 years,

---

[1] In addition to an annuity, it should not be forgotten that the spenddown money can also be used towards purchasing non-countable items, such as a vehicle, prepaid funeral, home repairs, furniture, etc.

or nine years, 7 months. Therefore, the annuity she purchases must be for a term lasting nine years, seven months or less. In New Hampshire, the relevant life expectancy tables can be found at the end of Section 400 of a publication known as the Adult Assistance Manual. The life expectancy tables used in Massachusetts can be found in the "Actuarial Life Table" section of the Social Security Administration website.

2.   The SPIA contract needs to state that it is irrevocable, non-assignable, and has no cash surrender value. In other words, the contract cannot be cashed in for a lump sum, and cannot be sold for cash to a third party.

3.   The SPIA needs to name the state as the primary beneficiary of the annuity, to the extent of Medicaid benefits paid, should the Community Spouse die before the annuity is all paid out. For example, let's continue with the example of Helen. Helen purchases a five-year annuity. (Recall that the term can be as long as nine years, seven months, but it can be less.) If Helen lives for the entire five-year term, then she will have been paid back all of her money plus interest, and the annuity contract will come to an end. However, say Helen passes away after year number four, so that one year's worth of payments remain to be paid under the contract. These remaining payments need to go to the state, as reimbursement for the Medicaid benefits paid for Helen's husband.

Although the SPIA can protect most, if not all of the spend-down money, it has two drawbacks. First is the risk that the Community Spouse would himself or herself later need to go into a nursing home while the SPIA is still in force. In this event, the annuity payments will have to be spent on his or her care. Second, as explained above, there is the risk that the Community Spouse dies before the annuity is all paid out. In this case, the remaining payments due need to go to the state, to the extent of Medicaid benefits paid for the nursing home spouse.

In our view, however, the benefits of the SPIA greatly outweigh the disadvantages, because the Community Spouse is completely protected from the devastating effects of the Medicaid spenddown. He or she can keep just about all of the assets, and can still maintain his or her financial dignity.

B. Unmarried People

Crisis Medicaid Planning for unmarried people can also be done, though the options are more limited than they are for married people. There are two options available to unmarried people.

1. Gift Trust

For people with sufficient assets to cover the five-year Medicaid lookback, a legal technique known as a "Gift Trust" can be used to protect assets. With a Gift Trust, you keep on hand sufficient funds to cover your expenses for five years, and gift the rest of the funds to your children or other trusted heirs. They, in turn, put these funds into an irrevocable trust. At the end of five years, you would qualify for Medicaid and the assets in the Gift Trust will be safe. A simple example will make this clear. Denise, age 82, is widowed and has a total estate of $850,000. She has just entered a nursing home, and her monthly budget is as follows:

Social Security benefits	$1,300.00
Pension benefits	500.00
Nursing Home	(9,500.00)
Medicare Supplement	(275.00)
Medicare Part D	(50.00)
Net outflow	-$8,025.00

With a net outflow of $8,025.00 per month, it will cost approximately $481,500 to cover the five-year lookback. Given that Denise has an estate of $850,000, she keeps on hand the $481,500 that she needs to cover her expenses, and she puts $368,500 into the Gift Trust. At the end of five years, she will be eligible for Medicaid, and the money in the Gift Trust will be protected. At Denise's death, the Gift Trust will terminate and will be distributed to her heirs.

This is the simplest of examples, and we are using it just to illustrate how the Gift Trust works. In a real case, we would need to take into account the effects of inflation over the five-year period and possible tax consequences on liquidating or changing title on assets. However, in the right case, a Gift Trust can be used to protect a significant amount of assets.

2. Immediate Annuity

Another type of Medicaid Planning technique involves the same type of immediate annuity that we use in the case of a married couple. Take the example of Peter, who is 80 years old, unmarried and has three adult children. He has an estate of $150,000 and has just entered a nursing home. His income of $1,250 is composed of Social Security of $750 and a pension of $500. The nursing home costs $10,000 per month and he pays $250 for his Medicare Supplement insurance. If he were simply to pay the monthly bill, his net out-of-pocket cost would be as follows:

Nursing home	$10,000.00
Medicare Supplement	250.00
Less Income	(1,250.00)
Out of Pocket	$9,000.00

At this rate, Peter will be completely out of funds in about 17 months. Instead of simply spending down, he puts his $150,000 into an eight-year immediate annuity. The annuity will pay him approximately $1,600 per month.

After he purchases the annuity, his assets will be such that he will be eligible for Medicaid. His monthly income will be $2,850, being composed of Social Security of $750, a pension of $500 and his annuity payment of $1,600. After deducting his Medicare Supplement insurance of $250 and his personal needs allowance of $70, he will pay the nursing home $2,530. Medicaid will pay the rest. By purchasing the annuity, he has reduced his monthly out of pocket expenses from $9,000 to $2,530.

Additionally, he has increased the chances of leaving an inheritance to his children. Here's why: The state pays the nursing home much less than the private pay rate. In fact, the so-called "Medicaid Rate" is usually about half of what a private paying patient pays. The state also gets credit for the patient's monthly contribution to the nursing home. If the Medicaid Rate of Peter's nursing home is $6,000 per month, and if he pays the nursing home $2,530, the state will only pay $3,470. If Peter dies prior to the eight-year term of the annuity, the state will be entitled to be reimbursed from the remaining annuity proceeds to the extent it has paid Medicaid benefits on his behalf. Any remaining funds in the annuity will go to Peter's children. Whether or not there will be money left for the children depends on how long Peter will live. However, had Peter not purchased the annuity, the chances that his children would have received an inheritance would have been very low. With the annuity, the chances improve dramatically.

Chapter 8
Special Medicaid Issues Posed by Second Marriages

Most of our clients are familiar with this verse from an old Frank Sinatra song:

Love is lovelier, the second time around.
Just as wonderful, with both feet on the ground.
It's that second time you hear your love song sung.
Makes you think, perhaps, that love, like youth,
is wasted on the young.

As this American popular standard points out, marriages later in life can indeed be more satisfying the "second time around." This must be true, judging from the high rate at which our clients get married for the second time. Very often, marrying for a second time in retirement years makes people seem more energetic, vibrant, and alive. It gives them a fresh outlook on life, and can even, it seems, make them live longer.

Yet, what can be a blessing to most people in second marriages can quickly become a curse if one of them enters a nursing home. Take the example of Harold and Betty, both in their eighties, married for a second time, and both with grown children from their first marriages. Here are their assets:

Harold		**Betty**	
House	$250,000	Beach house	$300,000
CDs	100,000	CDs	25,000
Savings	10,000	Savings	30,000

About six years ago, Betty was diagnosed with Alzheimer's Disease and Harold has been taking care of her at home. Betty's condition has lately become much worse, and Harold's doctor told him that his own health would begin to suffer unless Betty goes into a nursing home.

Harold enjoys doing yard work and the odd jobs necessary to maintain a house. He is still physically active and healthy, and things like mowing the lawn, painting, gardening and shoveling snow get him fresh air and exercise. As he puts it, "Puttering around the house keeps me young." Unfortunately, Betty's condition has become such that she has started to require constant care, and Harold no longer has enough time to do the chores that he so much likes to do. Therefore, they moved out of the house a year ago and signed a two-year lease on an apartment. Harold has not sold the house, however, and has left it vacant because it has come down from his first wife's side of the family, and he wants his children to inherit it when he passes away.

Before getting married, Harold and Betty signed a premarital agreement, which essentially says that Harold's assets go to his two children on his death, and Betty's assets go to her two children. The agreement also says that Harold and Betty are going to keep their assets separate, and that each is not going to be responsible for the other's debts and obligations. Betty's children, in particular, are concerned about the beach house, which they all love, and which has increased in value dramatically over the years. Much of Harold's money, including the house, was inherited from his first wife's side of the family, and Harold's children do not want to see their father lose these assets for the care of Betty, who is largely a stranger to them.

Harold, accompanied by his two children, goes to see an Elder Law Attorney, and asks for the attorney's help in qualifying Betty for Medicaid as soon as possible. He gives the attorney a copy of a durable power of attorney that Betty signed, naming him as her Agent. What issues are presented here? Let's see what would happen if Harold were to do nothing. Although Harold is worried about loss of his assets, he is not overly concerned. He and Betty paid a reputable lawyer good money to write a premarital agreement, which says that their assets and debts are separate. The lawyer assured them that the premarital agreement was valid and enforceable. Well, Harold is in for a very rude surprise. While a premarital agreement is enforceable as to inheritance and divorce issues, it is decidedly *not* enforceable when it comes to nursing homes and Medicaid. This is because a premarital agreement is made under the authority of state law. Medicaid, as we have seen in earlier chapters, is based on federal law, and federal law supersedes any contrary state law. Therefore, the Elder Law Attorney advises Harold, much to his astonishment, that the premarital agreement might as well not even exist. For Medicaid purposes, it has no force at all. This is the first lesson for people who marry later in life. Premarital agreement or not, or whether they keep their assets separate or not, when the couple says, "I do," for Medicaid purposes, they have consented to make their assets available to the other one's nursing home costs. For the couple involved in the second marriage, then, some form of asset protection is essential. Generally speaking, such a couple should seriously consider an Irrevocable Medicaid Trust.

Let's get back to Harold. The attorney gives Harold and his children a minute to get over their shock, and then presents the following, rather grim analysis: Both Harold's house and Betty's house are countable assets, because the rule that the Community Spouse's house is a non-countable asset only applies if the house is used as his or her homestead. Recall that while Harold owns the house, he does not live in it. Therefore, it loses its status as a non-countable asset and becomes a fully countable asset. Betty's beach house is also countable, for the same reason. (Note that if Harold lived in his house, it would not be countable, while Betty's house would be countable in any event, since there is no protection for second houses.) The attorney explains that Harold is allowed to keep half of the assets, up to a cap of $120,900 (or the first $120,900 in Massachusetts), Betty can keep $2,500 worth of assets, ($2,000 in Massachusetts) and the rest of the assets need to be spent down before Betty is eligible for Medicaid. The fact that Harold's house and most of his money were inherited from his first wife is completely irrelevant.

After giving Harold and his children this bad news, the Elder Law Attorney goes on to discuss possible solutions. If Harold wants to qualify Betty for Medicaid immediately, then he can keep his $120,900, sell his house, have Betty sell her house, and put the proceeds into an immediate annuity from which Harold will derive the income. Assuming that the annuity is set up to comply with the legal requirements we have seen in another chapter, then Betty will qualify for Medicaid.

What are the issues raised by this solution? First, Harold will need to sell the house that he always wanted his children to inherit and he will forever lose any chance of doing the yard work and tinkering that he loves. Betty's children will also lose the beach house. Worse, the proceeds of the sale of Betty's beach house, as well as her savings and CDs, will, through the annuity, be payable to Harold. This result will completely violate their intention, as expressed in the premarital agreement, of keeping their assets separate! The inheritance that Betty intended for her children will go to Harold through the annuity, and, when he dies, this money will go to Harold's children. Betty's children, the attorney explains, are the beneficiaries of the premarital agreement. If Harold goes the annuity route, Betty's children might even be able to sue Harold, or Harold's children, for breach of the premarital agreement. Harold, like most people of his generation, is scrupulously honest, and has a rock-solid belief in keeping his commitments. Thus, he would not even consider taking Betty's money, and the thought of being sued by her children sends chills up his spine.

There is another issue that affects people in this position. In most cases, the children of people involved in second marriages are strangers to one another. Very often, they live in different states, they only met at the wedding, and, at best, they see each other once a year at Christmas or Thanksgiving. But for the fact that their parents are married, they have nothing in common with each other. As the case of Harold and Betty illustrates, these children have very different interests from each other, and, more often than not, what is good for one side of the family is bad for the other. A great deal of resentment and hostility can build up if a child's expected inheritance is lost to pay for the nursing home care of someone who is very nearly a stranger.

Recall from an earlier chapter that a requirement of getting Medicaid for a married couple is a Resource Assessment. The Resource Assessment is a detailed list of all of the assets of both spouses as of the date the ill spouse is institutionalized.

Let's go back to our Harold and Betty example, but let's change the facts somewhat. Say that Harold no longer has any interest in managing his finances and has turned over management to his adult children. Prior to Betty getting Medicaid, she has to do a Resource Assessment. She needs the cooperation of Harold's children. However, Harold's children are no friend of Betty, and they do not cooperate in turning over Harold's records to the Medicaid agency. Therefore, the Resource Assessment cannot get done, and Betty cannot get the Medicaid benefits that she needs. Obviously, we have quite a problem, and one without a good solution.

In writing this chapter, it was not our intention to discourage people from getting married later in life. It was our intention, however, to alert people to the pitfalls and "traps for the unwary" that can await them if one of them gets sick and needs nursing home care later on. How can people thinking about getting married protect themselves and their children? When contemplating marriage, a visit to an Elder Law Attorney is essential, as it can prevent the very real "parade of horribles" that we have recited above.

First, a premarital agreement is a must. As we have seen, such an agreement will have no affect whatsoever on sheltering assets from the nursing home. However, a premarital agreement can deal with other important issues, such as inheritance rights, separate ownership of assets, and property settlements in the event of divorce. Of course, such an agreement isn't very romantic, but, as the song with which we opened this chapter states, second love is "Just as wonderful [but] with both feet on the ground." Older people, having had a whole lifetime of experience, know that marriage, in addition to being about love, has serious financial overtones, as well. A premarital agreement deals with those unpleasant, but necessary, financial issues.

Second, to avoid the Harold and Betty situation, people contemplating second marriages can put in place the Medicaid Trust that we visited in an earlier chapter. This trust is an excellent way of protecting both monetary assets and real estate. You can live in the house, and you can sell it, if you want to do so. After the five-year waiting period for the trust has expired, the trust assets will be safe.

In the second marriage context, the Medicaid Trust can be crucial. Say that Betty and Harold had each established such a trust at the time of their marriage. When Betty had to go into a nursing home, both sets of assets would have been protected. Betty would have qualified for Medicaid immediately, and neither Betty nor Harold would have lost anything. Just as significantly, relations between their children would have remained friendly. For these reasons, anyone contemplating a second marriage should consider a Medicaid Trust as a standard estate planning tool.

Chapter 9
Putting Assets into Children's Names

A common Medicaid planning technique involves putting assets, such as a house or bank account, into the names of your adult children. If done properly, with the safeguards described later in this chapter, re-titling the house or other real estate can be an effective Medicaid planning technique. However, if done improperly, it can be a disaster waiting to happen. The example of the family home is easiest to understand, and, therefore, we will concentrate on that. The first part of this chapter will look at a situation where assets are simply put into children's names without any safeguards, and the second part of the chapter will examine how to do it safely.

1. *Putting the House into the Children's Names Without any Safeguards*

Putting the house, or any other asset, into the names of your children without any safeguards is a very dangerous thing to do. Generally speaking, it should almost never be done. There are four reasons for this.

A. Liability

Any asset put into the names of your children is subject to their liabilities. So, if your house is in your daughter's name and she gets divorced, it can easily become part of her property settlement. Or let's say your daughter gets sued. Her creditors can put an attachment on your house. Or, if your son - or his wife- gets very ill and needs nursing home care, then your assets, which are in his name, will need to be spent on his or his wife's care.

B. Loss of Control

If you put your assets into your adult children's names, you lose control over those assets. For example, say your house is in your son's name, and you want to sell it. You need to ask his permission, because, legally it is his house. This is not a very good position to be in, because what if he can't, or won't, give you the permission you need? For example, perhaps he is being sued by his creditors, and there is an attachment on the house. Or say he does give you permission to sell, and you do so. Within a year, he files bankruptcy. In this situation, your house, or the proceeds of the sale, can be pulled into his bankruptcy case.

Here is a tragic example that happens from time to time. Say your son marries a woman you simply can't stand. Your house is in your son's name, and he comes down with a serious illness and dies before you. He has a will leaving his assets (including your house) to his wife. She is now your landlord. Obviously, you do not want to find yourself in this situation.

C. Tax Problems

Putting any appreciated asset, especially your house or stock, into your adult child's name can, in two situations, cause him or her to pay unnecessary capital gains taxes. First, say you want to sell the house. In most cases, you will not pay capital gains taxes when you sell your primary homestead. However, even if the house is in your adult child's name, it is your homestead, not his. Thus, if the house is sold, your child is not entitled to the capital gains exclusion, and any gain will be subject to capital gains taxes.

Second, if you put your house in your child's name during life, then he or she is not able to take advantage of the stepped-up tax basis at your death. In other words, if your child had inherited your house at death, instead of having it put in his name during life, then most, if not all, capital gains would have been avoided when the house is later sold. However, if the house is put into your child's name during your life, this important tax advantage is lost, and our children can be subject to unnecessary capital gains taxes.

D. RSA 151:E-19

Recall our earlier discussion of the Fiduciary Liability statute, enacted in New Hampshire in July 2013. If you put assets into your childrens' names and need to apply for Medicaid within five-years, this law can lead to nasty consequences. Any asset put into your children's name is subject to a five-year Medicaid lookback. If you apply for Medicaid within the five years and are denied benefits, then the nursing home can sue your children for the value of the assets you have put in their names. So, not only does the transfer of the assets disqualify you from Medicaid, it leaves your children susceptible to being sued. Rather than take this risk, putting the asset into the Medicaid Trust is the much safer choice.

2. Putting the House in your Children's Names With the Proper Safeguards

The Medicaid Trust is, in our opinion, the best way by far to shelter real estate. However, with appropriate safeguards, a change of title to your children's names could also work.

A. Life Estate Deed

A Life Estate is a legal right to live in a home owned by another person. If you deed your house to your children, you can put language in the deed reserving a life estate, *i.e.*, the deed can say that you have lifetime use and occupancy of the home. Although this transfer is subject to a five-year lookback period for Medicaid, the basic advantage of the life estate is that you are assured of being able to live in the property despite your children's death, divorce, or bankruptcy. You continue to live in the house during your life, and on death, the house goes to your children without probate. When the children inherit the house, they receive a stepped-up tax basis, which will minimize, if not eliminate any capital gains taxes when they sell the property.

However, there are two primary disadvantages of a life estate deed. First, as mentioned above, it is subject to the five-year lookback period. For this reason, in New Hampshire, the children who receive the house would be subject to lawsuit under NH RSA 151:E-19. Second, you lose control of the house, so that if you want to sell it, you need to get your children's permission. This can be an awkward position to be in. They might decline to give that permission. When the property is sold, the proceeds are split between you and your children, pursuant to Medicaid and IRS formulas. Your portion of the proceeds would likely be sheltered from capital gains taxes, but your children's portion would not.

B. Deeds With Special Power of Appointment

To eliminate the problems with life estate deeds, you can include a "Special Power of Appointment" (SPA) provision in the deed. By use of the SPA, your children would have an ownership interest in the house, but you reserve the right to take their ownership interest away from them. Using the SPA, you would be able to redistribute the ownership of the house among your other children, grandchildren or other relatives if you want to do so. The SPA provision in the deed would say something like this:

> I hereby grant to my children, Andy, Michael and Suzy, as joint tenants with right of survivorship, the following described real estate at 100 Main Street, Anytown, New Hampshire (or Massachusetts). I hereby reserve the power, exercisable as often as I may choose, by an instrument recorded at the registry of deeds during my lifetime, to appoint the premises herein conveyed, outright or upon such trusts, conditions or limitations as I may specify,

> to any one or more of my issue or the spouses of
> my issue.

This language allows you to have almost total control over the property. If any of your children are sued, get divorced, marry someone you do not like, go bankrupt, become estranged from the family, or if there is some other unforeseen change in circumstances, you can eliminate his or her share of the property. Alternatively, you can set up their ownership in trust or otherwise put "strings" on their ownership. The SPA gives you the security of knowing that your house is protected from long-term care, while giving you control over it, and giving you flexibility in dealing with future changes. Keep in mind, however, that the five-year lookback applies, as does RSA 151:E-19 in New Hampshire.

As you can see, there are various ways of protecting your assets, and particularly your house from being lost to long-term care. You can use the Medicaid Trust, or a Life Estate Deed, or a Special Power of Apointment deed. As we have said many times throughout this book, there is no single correct answer for everyone. You need to analyze your goals, your situation, and your family's situation, and choose the alternative which is best suited for you and your family.

Chapter 10
Federal and Massachusetts
Estate Taxes

When someone dies, his or her estate may be subject to a tax known as the "Estate Tax." Generally, all of the assets that a deceased person either owned or had a legal interest in at the time of death are subject to estate taxes, as are gifts over a certain amount that the person made during life. If the total of the assets owned at death plus the gifts are above a certain threshold, then the estate tax is imposed, and if the assets are below that threshold, there is no tax.

Certain deductions against the tax are allowed, including debts, expenses of administering the estate such as legal and accounting fees, charitable bequests, and assets passing either to the surviving spouse or to certain types of trusts for the benefit of the surviving spouse. If a tax is due, it must be paid within nine months from the date of death. Starting in 2017, the threshold for Federal Estate Tax is $5.49 million per individual. In other words, a person can leave $5.49 million to his or her heirs and pay no federal estate tax. According to a 2015 report from Congress's Joint Committee on Taxation, out of 2.6 million total deaths in the United States in 2013, the sum of 4,700 estate tax returns were filed showing a tax due. That means the estate tax hits roughly 0.2% of Americans, or 1 out of every 500 people who die. It is safe to say that none of our clients need worry about the Federal Estate Tax.

How about state estate taxes? New Hampshire residents get a break here, in that New Hampshire has no estate tax. Massachusetts, however, does have an estate tax. The Massachusetts estate tax is a graduated tax, *i.e.*, the bigger the estate, the higher the tax. Here is a simple chart which can be used to estimate the tax:

Size of Estate	Tax Rate
$1,000,000	0.00%
$1,000,001	3.32%
$1,500,000	4.29%
$2,000,000	4.98%
$2,000,001	4.98%
$2,500,000	5.52%
$3,000,000	6.07%
$3,500,000	6.55%
$4,000,000	7.01%
$5,120,000	7.91%
$5,250,000	8.01%
$5,340,000	8.08%

To determine whether or not a Massachusetts estate tax return is required for your estate, your executor will have to calculate the value of your gross estate. Whether or not the assets avoid probate is irrelevant to the calculation. The estate includes, but is not limited to, the following:

1. Real estate, both inside and outside of Massachusetts;
2. Bank accounts;
3. Investment accounts;
4. Stocks and bonds;
5. Annuities;
6. IRAs and 401ks;
7. Vehicles;
8. Household possessions; and/or
9. Life insurance proceeds

With proper planning, a married couple can double the estate tax exemption from $1 million to $2 million. This is done by way of a "Dual Revocable Trust" estate plan, which includes an individual trust for each spouse. The trusts are each funded with approximately half of the total estate. After the death of the first spouse, his or her trust assets are allocated into two separate sub-trusts, the so-called "A-B Trust." The first sub-trust, funded with up to the amount of $1 million, is known as the "Bypass Trust," or "Family Trust." Under the Family Trust, assets are available to the surviving spouse and the children (but principally the surviving spouse) for health, maintenance, education and support. In this way, the trust assets can be used for the support of the surviving spouse, but are held in a way that those assets are not part of his or her taxable estate. The rest of the assets belonging to the trust of the first spouse to die pass into another sub-trust called the "Marital Trust." The Marital Trust provides the surviving spouse with all of the income. It also often gives the trustee discretion to distribute principal as necessary for the surviving spouse's maintenance and health. Alternatively, the surviving spouse can choose to receive the assets outright. Unlike the Family Trust, the Marital Trust is a part of the surviving spouse's taxable estate. In other words, when the second spouse dies, the Marital Trust assets are included among the assets that are subject to estate taxes. However, the Marital Trust is not taxed at the death of the first spouse, since it is subject to the 100% Marital Deduction. Upon the surviving spouse's death, the assets left in the Family Trust and Marital Trust pass to the heirs. The Family Trust is distributed tax free.

There are two different ways that the Family Trust and Marital Trust are funded. One way is called "formula funding." With formula funding, the executor does not have any discretion, since he or she is required, based on a predetermined formula, to allocate the assets among both trusts. The formula typically states that the trusts are funded in such a way as to make sure that there is no tax at the first death. The second way is known as "Disclaimer Funding." With disclaimer funding, the decision as to how to fund the trusts is made by the surviving spouse. He or she "disclaims," or refuses to receive, assets of his or her choice. These disclaimed assets pass to the Family Trust. The assets not disclaimed go to the Marital Trust, or can go directly to the spouse.

Under the A-B type of estate plan, there are no estate taxes at the first death, and at the second death, estate taxes are either eliminated or minimized. A simple example will show how this plan works. Say that Bill and Myra have an estate of $2 million, and say that Bill dies first. They each have a simple will that leaves all of the assets to the surviving spouse. When Bill dies, his will leaves all of his assets to Myra. An estate tax return will be filed, since Bill's estate is over the $1 million threshold. No tax will be due, though, since the money being left to Myra is subject to the Marital Deduction; *i.e.*, it is deducted from the estate tax. Some years later Myra dies, having an estate of $2 million. A tax of approximately $100,000 will be due on the entire estate.

To avoid this result and minimize estate taxes, Bill and Myra enter into A-B trusts. Each trust is funded with half the estate, or $1 million. At Bill's death, no estate tax return is due, and his $1 million goes into the Family Trust. Myra has $1 million in her own right and she can draw on Bill's money if necessary. At Myra's death, she has $1 million. Her estate is not taxed, and neither is Bill's. Therefore, the sum of $100,000 in taxes has been entirely avoided. This is the simplest of possible examples, and the situation is usually more complex. However, the example makes the point that by using two trusts, the tax exemption can be doubled, and tens of thousands of dollars can be saved from taxation.

Chapter 11
Trusts For Children With Special Needs

Some of our clients have children with special needs. Frequently, the special need is a physical, mental or developmental disability. Where these children are receiving government assistance, such as Medicaid or SSI, it is imperative that parents plan their estates very carefully. If the estate is structured incorrectly, an inheritance otherwise designated for a child with special needs may actually disqualify him or her from government assistance. In addition, a great many families are affected by an adult child who is addicted to opiates or other drugs, or to alcohol or gambling. While we do not need to be concerned about a loss of government benefits in such a case, an inheritance to such a child can certainly be a risk. Finally, many parents are concerned about children who do not have a disability or addiction, but who simply lack good judgment, or who are not good money managers. Perhaps the adult child spends beyond his or her means, or incurs significant credit card debt, or is in an unstable marriage. In such a case, parents are often fearful that the inheritance will be frittered away. These are real-life problems that affect countless families, and which require special attention and expertise.

A. Special Needs Trusts for Children With Disabilities

An outright inheritance to a child with a disability is at risk to being lost to the state or may disqualify the child for governmental assistance. This is simply not an acceptable result for people who want to provide "extras" to their child with disabilities, *i.e.*, to supplement, but not to replace, benefits to which their child is eligible to receive as a result of his or her disability.

To qualify for many governmental programs, a child with disabilities may not have countable assets of over $2,000. So, if a married couple with $300,000 in total assets leaves those assets equally among their two children, Sam and Mike, each will receive $150,000. Sam can use his inheritance however he wants. Mike, who is disabled and is receiving government benefits, will see his inheritance used to reimburse the government for any aid he has received. If there is any money left after he has repaid the government, he will need to spend it down. In essence, this family's estate plan is flawed, because Mike, for all practical purposes, has been disinherited.

Throughout the years, we have seen people try all sorts of self-help type approaches to solving this dilemma. It is common for the family referred to above to leave Mike's $150,000 to Sam, with Sam making an unwritten promise to use the money for Mike's care. While this may seem to work, it can cause disastrous consequences, such as:

- Sam dies before Mike, and leaves his entire estate (including Mike's $150,000) to his wife, who then remarries;
- Sam's wife divorces him, and claims that Mike's $150,000, which Sam is holding, is part of the marital assets, subject to equal division;
- Sam is responsible for a major auto accident for which he is not adequately insured, and the injured party sues;
- Sam or his wife suffer from a catastrophic illness or injury, and need to go to a nursing home; and/or
- Sam has to fill out a student aid form for his college-age child, only to realize that Mike's $150,000 is really Sam's asset for financial aid purposes.

Murphy's Law being what it is, there are many things that can go wrong and that can deprive Mike of his inheritance. All of these things could have been avoided through careful planning by Sam and Mike's parents. They could have used a "Special Needs Trust," also known as a "Supplemental Needs Trust," in their estate planning.

A Special Needs Trust (SNT) comes in a variety of forms, and can be used by both married and unmarried people.

- There are stand-alone SNTs, which are separate from your other trust;
- There are SNTs that are a part of, and included with, your other trust; such a SNT is funded and becomes effective at your death;
- There are SNTs which are set up as part of a will, these SNTs are subject to the disadvantages of probate, discussed earlier;

- There are SNTs which are designed to supplement or augment governmental benefits;
- There are revocable SNTs;
- There are irrevocable SNTs; and
- There are SNTs that are designed to provide for the total, or nearly total, support of the special needs child.

A discussion of each type of trust is way beyond the scope of this book, but we think that a brief overview would be helpful.

The stand-alone SNT is designed to operate independently of the other parts of the parents' estate plan. It is a separate trust for the benefit of the disabled child. It is often funded by a life insurance policy on the parents' lives. An advantage of this type of trust is that a grandparent or other relative may add or gift property to the trust at any time, whether before or after the parents' deaths.

A more common SNT is one which is incorporated within an existing trust. Upon the death of both parents, the share intended for their disabled child does not go directly to him or her, but continues to be held in further trust for his or her benefit. Since this type of SNT does not come into existence until the parents' deaths, it may not be added to during the parents' lives by well-meaning relatives.

The most common type of SNT is one for supplemental care. This trust is designed to supplement, but not to take the place, of government benefits, and guarantees funds for the "extras," over and above what modest government benefits provide.

A less common type of SNT is a general support trust. This type of trust is designed for the beneficiary's total support.

Because the cost of a lifetime of care is so expensive, these types of SNTs are not done that often.

With a Revocable SNT, the parents have the right to put money in or take money out at any time. The drawback to this type of trust is that if the parents need nursing home care, the trust assets are countable, and would need to be spent down. This trust is also subject to creditor claims. For these reasons, it is far less certain that the trust assets will be there for the disabled child.

Finally, there are Irrevocable SNTs. In these cases, the parents give up ownership and control of the trust assets and cannot amend the trust if circumstances change. However, it is certain that the assets will be there for the special needs child, even if the parents need nursing home care or are sued by creditors.

As the above examples show, there is no one-size-fits-all SNT. Careful analysis is needed to ensure that you use the correct type for your child and your family circumstances.

Although there are many different types of SNTs, they all give the trustee extensive discretion as to how to make distributions for the beneficiary. In the supplemental care SNT, for example, it is common to allow for the following types of expenditures:

- Medical and dental expenses;
- Clothing;
- Transportation;
- Dietary needs; and/or
- Trips and entertainment.

This is not an exhaustive list by any means, but it highlights some of the items that a well-drafted SNT will contain.

Often, the trust will require the trustee to:

- Make regular visits to the beneficiary;
- Arrange for medical and dental exams;
- Evaluate the education and training programs which are available to the beneficiary;
- Determine the appropriateness of residential opportunities available to the beneficiary; and/or
- Determine whether the beneficiary is entitled to public assistance.

The choice of a trustee is crucial. Sometimes, a co-trustee arrangement is appropriate. In such a case, a bank or trust company acts as the "financial" trustee, or a corporate trustee and a family member acts as a "personal" trustee. The personal trustee looks to the financial trustee for funds to pay what the personal trustee feels is necessary or desirable for the beneficiary.

Trusts for Children with Other Special Needs, Such as Mental Health Issues, Substance Misuse or Gambling Issues

If an adult child has a mental health, drug, alcohol or gambling addiction, a bad marriage, an IRS problem, or is simply a poor money manager, the parents can establish a "Spendthrift" Trust. These trusts are designed to protect their child's inheritance, not from the state, but from the child himself or herself, or from divorcing spouses or creditors. Spendthrift Trusts are created as part of the parents' estate plan, and are incorporated within their trust to limit what the child receives, or to put conditions on what he or she receives. These trusts can stretch the child's inheritance over time, so a lump sum is not available for him to lose, or for creditors to take. Such a trust can give the trustee (usually a sibling) authority to distribute income and/or principal for the health, maintenance, education and support of the child and his or her family. Some trusts limit distribution to income only. Some allow for income and some percentage of principal to be distributed periodically. Such a trust can be flexible enough to allow the trustee to invest the child's share in an annuity, payable monthly over the child's lifetime. This protects the trustee from being pestered for distributions.

Chapter 12
Digital Assets

Up until a few years ago, a person's estate consisted entirely of paper records. These records would usually be collected in a safe place in the home or in a safe deposit box where the family would be able to easily find them after the person's death. Missing items did not usually present a problem, because they could be identified through account statements that arrived later in the mail.

However, these days, things are much different. Many of us have what are known as "digital assets." Digital assets include online bank and investment accounts, email accounts, picture and video storage sites, social networking sites such as Facebook and Twitter, as well as paperless billing for credit cards, utilities, auto insurance and loans. Sometimes valuable assets exist solely in the digital world, *e.g.*, virtual wallets like Paypal, frequent flier miles, and entire libraries of music and e-books. To complicate things, digital information is usually stored on a variety of devices, such as desktop or laptop computers, smartphones and tablets, e-readers, cameras and flash drives. Given that each of these accounts and devices have their own usernames, passwords and security questions and answers, the amount of digital data we have, as well as the ability to access it, can quickly become overwhelming.

These digital accounts and devices, and the information they contain can be extremely valuable. Yet, very few people have organized their digital information. This can make managing and accessing these assets very difficult after the person has died or become incapacitated. Worse, it can lead to an inability to locate the accounts or information, which can then become lost or, after a number of years, be deemed abandoned and go to the state. Many people have lost money because their children did not know about an online debt or they did not know about overdue bill payments because the notices were sent only by e-mail. Sometimes, children know about an overdue bill, but are unable to pay it without the online banking username and password. To make matters worse, trying to call and get information from a customer service representative can be a time-consuming exercise in frustration.

Although many digital assets are not inherently valuable, such as e-mail, Facebook or Twitter accounts, some have emotional value. Instead of having bulky photo albums and reels of eight millimeter movie film, people often use digital means for preserving this material. Without telling family members that these assets exist, and without telling them how to get access to them, there is a very significant risk that a lifetime of memories can be lost forever.

Therefore, anyone with digital assets — which is almost everyone these days — needs to give thought to preparing a "digital estate plan." The rights of trustees, executors, power of attorney holders, and beneficiaries with regard to digital assets are very unclear, because the law has not kept pace with technology. Although many web sites and online services have their own policies for how to deal with a user's death or incapacity, not all of them do. Even if an online service has a policy for these issues, as a practical matter, most people do not know what the policy says.

By creating a digital estate plan, you can help your family more easily locate, access and manage online accounts, determine if your digital property has any financial, emotional or historic value, and distribute or transfer any digital assets to the appropriate parties. In order to do this, you need to develop an inventory of these assets, including a list of how and where they are held, along with usernames, passwords, and answers to security questions. You can, and should, designate a "digital executor," who is a person (ideally a tech-savvy person) to manage these items. Doing this is not particularly difficult, but it does require thoroughness, organization and attention to detail. An ideal time to put this information together is when you are updating your estate plan.

Chapter 13
The Basic Building Blocks of a Financial Foundation for a Secure Retirement

When it comes to how to be positioned to enjoy a more worry-free retirement lifestyle, one that affords you financial independence, there are five common denominators of success. We have identified these factors based upon our having interviewed thousands of retirees over the past 20-plus years and observing what they had done to help ensure their success. These five steps are what we suggest in almost all situations. We suggest you consider these factors when planning for a solid foundation.

Emergency Reserve Fund: The first step is to determine your fixed monthly or annual expenses. We recommend creating a bank "buffer account" of cash containing 12 to 24 months of your fixed expenses. Maintaining this fund should allow you to get through anything unexpected without being forced to liquidate investments. Some people, especially those who like to invest, prefer to keep only a small amount of cash. The major risk of doing this is that you will lack sufficient liquid funds for emergencies or unexpected expenses during a period of market decline. We caution clients against doing this. Preservation of capital and maintaining flexibility are the main objective within this first goal.

Have no Debt: We suggest that, if possible, you enter retirement debt free. As part of your long-range planning, you should be saving for retirement while paying down on your debts such as mortgages, vehicle loans and the like. Doing so will reduce your monthly fixed expenses.

Have consistent income: Review your fixed monthly expenses against the amount of fixed monthly income coming in. Is there enough income coming in to manage the outflow? If not, your planning should involve tactics to increase your monthly cash inflow to offset your typical monthly outflow. For most people, the basic inflows come from Social Security and/or a defined benefit pension plan. Other techniques that should be reviewed for possible implementation include dividend income strategies, immediate annuity strategies and IRA draw-down strategies. The goal is to have enough income coming in on a predictable basis each month to manage most, if not all of your basic outflow. It is one thing to run out of money, but an entirely different thing to run out of lifetime income.

Build a well-rounded portfolio: After providing for a buffer account and determining how to derive sufficient monthly income to manage expenses, you should review your remaining financial assets and look to create a well-rounded portfolio to guard against inflation. Although the matrix of such a portfolio is beyond the scope of this chapter, typically a "well-rounded" portfolio would consist of equities, bonds and cash. Every person and situation is different, so everyone needs to construct a portfolio tailored to his or her lifetime needs.

Don't attempt to time the market: Over the years, we have watched people think they can outsmart the markets by selling and buying based on the news or on some event. While it can be tempting to do this, and while it may work once or twice, over a lifetime this behavior only loses. We suggest building and maintaining whatever portfolio design you determine best suits your needs. Do not allow a short-sighted emotional decision to have lifetime consequences.

Chapter 14
Long Term Care Insurance Planning Considerations – A Defense Against IRA Spend Down

In the right case, Long-Term Care Insurance can help protect you from the catastrophic expenses associated with a long-term nursing home stay. This type of insurance will help pay for the costs of a nursing home provided certain policy conditions are met. The policy provisions that will trigger the payments are inability to perform at least two so-called Activities of Daily Living (ADLs). The typical ADLs are eating, bathing, dressing, using the bathroom, continence, and transferring to and from bed. Failing the ADLs usually requires the certification from a physician.

There are many decisions that need to be considered when researching making a purchase of Long term Care insurance. These include:

1. Your Age: the older you are the more a policy will cost;
2. Daily or monthly Benefit Amount: With the average cost of a nursing home stay ranging $330 to $400 per day, you will want to pick a daily or monthly benefit

amount that covers the cost of the average. Keep in mind that not all people will need to cover 100% of the cost if they receive a pension benefit or Social Security;

3. Elimination Period: This is the amount of time required prior to the policy beginning to make payments. Most policies have 0, 90, 120, or even 180 day elimination periods prior to the commencement of the benefits. The most popular choice among brokers and policy holders is 90 days. This is meant to coordinate with Medicare, which typically pays for up to the first 100 days of nursing home confinement;

4. Length of Benefit: Most policies will pay for as little as two years and as long as a lifetime of benefit. The average stay in a nursing home is approximately two and a half years. At $11,000 to $12,000 per month, the typical nursing home stay will cost about $330,000. Therefore, choosing the proper length of benefit is a crucial decision; and

5. Inflation Protection: The daily rate of a nursing home stay continues to rise faster than the general cost of living. One method to protect against the future cost of the nursing home is to add an inflation rider to the policy. The inflation rider is usually five percent per year. Depending on your age and other financial circumstances, this inflation protection is a very important "add-on" to a long term care policy.

There are drawbacks to consider when researching long-term care insurance. First, many people simply cannot afford the premiums required to obtain this coverage. For many people, these premiums are simply out of reach and place too much pressure on their portfolio distribution rates.

The second drawback is that for most companies these premiums are "guaranteed renewable." This means once you have been approved for coverage, the insurance company can never drop you due to your health or age. However, they reserve the right to increase premiums on a "class" basis if approved by the state Insurance Department. These rate increases have occurred with some of the largest insurance companies in our country in the last several years, and some insurance carriers have eliminated selling long-term care insurance altogether. In other words, while the company must continue to insure you, your premiums can rise dramatically.

The third drawback and most common problem with purchasing long-term care insurance is the fact that the insurance companies review your health prior to making an offer to extend coverage. Many people simply cannot qualify for the coverage due to health issues.

There are several advantages for those who can qualify for long-term care insurance and who can afford the premiums. First, long term care coverage increases your choices for home health care, assisted care, and your choice of nursing home care. People who own long term care insurance enjoy financial peace of mind knowing you have dollars that will help cover the cost of a long-term care experience.

Second, there are strategies that you will have learned about in this book to protect your home, your cottage at the lake and your stocks, bonds, and cash. However, your retirement plans cannot be covered via these techniques and thus, will remain subject to nursing home spenddown. Long-term care insurance will afford you the ability to protect these retirement accounts which cannot be protected by traditional

Medicaid Planning techniques. This insurance coverage, when appropriately positioned as part of your estate plan, can significantly impact your ability to protect your assets for you and your family. Third, the volatility to which the long-term care marketplace has been exposed over the years has led to innovations in coverage design. Today, many policies are known as "hybrids." These policies provide life insurance death benefits *and* long term care insurance benefits within the same policy. This simply means that, one way or another, if the premiums have been paid over the years, the policy will eventually pay a benefit to your loved ones. This design can create a robust hedge against not only the potential costs for nursing home stays, but also can alleviate some of the drain created by taxes on an IRA.

Finally, it is important that you take the time to review whether long-term care insurance is feasible in your estate and financial planning situation. The appropriate placement of this coverage will avail you choice and time in implementing other planning strategies should a disability strike.

Chapter 15
Beyond Improved Cash Flow – Timing Your Social Security Decision

Most people understand the potential cash-flow benefits of delaying the onset of Social Security benefits from the age of 62 up to age 70. Each year of delay will increase the baseline monthly Social Security payment by about eight percent. Still, many people are focused on the "old school" conventional wisdom of taking Social Security benefits as soon as possible, becaue they are afraid of the government taking it away, or because they are afraid of it taking years to "break even" if they delay. These thoughts, however, are a bit near-sighted, and in this chapter we will explain a more productive approach.

You may have read about the benefit of the increased guaranteed cash-flow strategy that may occur if you delay the onset of your Social Security. Unfortunately, very few articles consider the improved long-term, tax-planning benefits associated with delayed benefits. Below are the advantages of using the delay strategy beyond just the improved lifetime income. The improved outcome, if managed correctly, can have a lifetime impact on cash flow, portfolio value, and retirement related monetary stress.

Let's discuss what many people think about when it comes to the timing of their Social Security Benefits. Taking benefits at age 62 may seem to be a logical way to enhance your monthly spendable income. Doing so may allow you to delay distributions from your retirement accounts and allow them to continue to grow on a tax-deferred basis. Sounds great, doesn't it?

An Unintended Consequence

If you delay the drawdown of your retirement accounts (we will call them IRAs for the remainder of this chapter), the IRAs can continue to compound on a tax-deferred basis. This can continue until you reach age 70½, when you are forced to start taking the Required Minimum Distributions. This sounds fine, but in doing so:

1. The IRA has most likely grown because no funds have yet been removed, causing the Required Distribution to be larger, due to the larger IRA year-end value. See IRS Publication 590 for life expectancy tables and distribution factors; and
2. If you or your spouse passes away, the survivor will no longer benefit from joint-filing tax status.

This creates what we call "bracket creep," which causes the surviving spouse to jump tax brackets. Married filers can earn a taxable income of $75,900 and be taxed in the 15 percent marginal bracket. Based on 2017 filing data, the figure for single clients is $37,950, or half of the joint amount.

Usually, spouses name each other as the primary beneficiary of each other's IRA accounts, and the survivor now holds 100 percent of the IRA portfolio. After the passing of one spouse, the survivor will likely go from the 15 percent marginal bracket to the next marginal bracket, 25 percent. They then usually fail the provisional income test for their Social Security Benefits. Now they have up to 85 percent of the reduced benefit (Social Security Survivor Benefit) taxed at the 25 percent federal income tax level for the rest of their life because of the reduced thresholds for single tax payers vs. joint taxpayers. We call this the "widow tax trap."

Fixing the Problem

How can you mitigate this dilemma? By delaying taking Social Security benefits if possible. With the ever-increasing Baby Boomer population living longer and longer, longevity planning is essential. You will not only enjoy the benefit of the annual increase in the future benefit caused by the delayed start of your Social Security benefit, you may also have room within your tax planning to begin drawing down your IRA at the wider joint filing status thresholds.

You can use this drawdown to live on, or if you do not need the funds, you can use the room within your tax bracket to convert them to Roth IRAs. This strategy will reduce the value of the traditional IRA portfolio over time, and thus reduce the eventual required minimum distribution amount. This strategy may also reduce the effects of the provisional income test on your Social Security benefits down the line. Roth IRAs have no required minimum distribution and distributions taken from them are tax-free.

Managing the distribution strategy or IRAs, in combination with the timing of Social Security benefits, can yield excellent cash-flow benefits for life and reduce the future tax burdens associated with deferring the drawdown of an IRA for too long. There are numerous strategies for making an impact on your long-range plans. This concept may not only increase your net after-tax cash flow for life, but it also yields a tax-free Roth IRA benefit for you and your loved ones.

Chapter 16
Qualified Plan Distribution Strategy: Net Unrealized Appreciation

Many retirees have accumulated very large 401(k) balances or other retirement plans as a result of a career's worth of savings. For some people, a large percentage of their retirement plan consists of highly-appreciated individual company stock. The tax savings you can generate using the Net Unrealized Appreciation (NUA) technique can make a significant impact on your financial and estate planning.

Unfortunately, many retirees and many advisors make a fundamental mistake: they roll over the retirement plan, which is rich in employer stock, to an IRA. Often, retirees and advisors assume rolling the plan into an IRA is the only option available. On the surface, this seems like the standard operating procedure. However, if you go this route, you may cost your family thousands of dollars in additional taxes they should not have to pay!

NUA Explained

NUA occurs when an employer-sponsored retirement plan allows the employee to purchase employer securities as part of the plan. When an employee retires, the IRS treats these securities held inside the plan differently than it treats other assets, such as cash and mutual funds. When the employee rolls over his or her retirement plan to an IRA, he or she may withdraw the employer securities and pay income tax based on the cost basis (not the current value) and capital gains tax on the gain if he or she sells the employer securities. Then, the cash, mutual funds, or other investment accounts will roll over to the IRA and are not taxed until withdrawn. (See IRS publication 575.)

Case study

Mr. Smith, age 65, has a 401(k) plan valued at $500,000, half in mutual funds and half in company stock. The cost basis of the company stock is $50,000. Assume Mr. Smith is in the 25% federal income tax bracket.

Option 1: Normal rollover approach

Mr. Smith rolls the entire account into an IRA. Any normal distributions he takes will be taxed in the 25% federal income tax bracket. At age 70½, he will be forced to take required minimum distributions and pay taxes on these distributions in his then applicable (assumed 25%) tax bracket. (See IRS Publication 590.)

Option 2: Net Unrealized Appreciation rollover approach

Mr. Smith rolls the stock out of the 401(k) plan. The cost basis of the stock is $50,000 and he must pay income tax on the cost basis of $12,500 ($50,000 x 25% tax rate). The stock is transferred to a non-qualified account, *i.e.* a non-retirement account. No additional taxes are owed on the stock until Mr. Smith sells them. If he sells the stock, he will pay capital gain tax on the sale, as opposed to ordinary income tax, and thus is taxed at 15% (capital gain tax is 0% if in the 15% bracket, 15% if up to the 25% bracket and no greater than 20% if above the 25% bracket based on 2017 IRS rates), not 25%. This creates an immediate tax savings of 10%. Shares sold under this technique are taxed at long-term capital gain tax rates (up to the NUA) regardless of the length of time between the roll-out and the sale of the stock and at short-or long-term capital gains rates on any additional gain beyond the NUA based on the time of sale. If he does not sell the stock, there are no additional taxes beyond the ordinary income tax due on the rollout. All other remaining funds are rolled to an IRA.

Benefits of Net Unrealized Appreciation
First, by utilizing the NUA approach you will reduce your overall tax burden on your 401(k) plan and have the opportunity to use capital gain tax rates vs. ordinary income tax on $200,000 of the value of the account. Second, by reducing the amount rolling into the IRA, you will reduce the required distribution amounts when you reach age 70½. Required Minimum Distributions (RMD) are calculated on the year-end balance of the IRA, and if you remove the value of the stock from the account it will not be included in the RMD calculation. Third, capital gain tax rates are significantly lower than the current income tax rates. These tax savings can be used to fund long-term care and other estate preservation strategies using funds that otherwise would have been lost to taxes!

Drawbacks of Net Unrealized Appreciation

This technique is designed primarily for those above age 59½. The early distribution penalties apply to those who elect this option under age 59½, and a 10% early distribution penalty will apply. The technique, however, may still be a viable option under these circumstances, as the penalty tax only pertains to the "basis" of the roll-out and not the full value of the stock.

NUA does not enjoy a stepped-up basis at death. When reviewing your overall estate planning objectives, you must be aware that, unlike other highly appreciated securities you may own, the NUA stock will not receive the increase to market value at death and may present a large capital gain tax to the beneficiary. A plan to liquidate out of the NUA stock may be necessary to prevent erosion due to the tax the beneficiary will pay.

If you were an active trader within the retirement plan, buying and selling the employer stock, the basis may be significantly affected. If the market value of the stock is close to the basis of the stock, the benefits of using the NUA approach will be minimal. Under these circumstances, most of the roll-out would be taxed as ordinary income. If you were not an active trader within your qualified plan a thorough review of this planning technique may protect you and your family from yet another major tax trap!

Chapter 17
Social Security Presents a Potential Tax Trap for the Uninformed.

In 1993, a modification to Social Security benefit taxation caused one of the largest tax increases to affect retirees in the history of our country. Very few retirees understood the significance of this change and even fewer are taking advantage of planning techniques to reduce or eliminate this increase.

Before 1993, seniors paid taxes on half of their Social Security benefits if their combined income was $25,000 for individuals or $32,000 for married couples. In 1993, the portion of taxable Social Security increased to 85 percent, and individuals with provisional incomes above $34,000 and married couples with provisional incomes above $44,000 were subject to the higher rate of taxation. Unmarried people with provisional incomes below $25,000 and married couples with provisional incomes below $32,000 pay no taxes on their Social Security benefits.

Simply explained, provisional income is the sum of a person's wages if still employed, interest on money, dividends on investments, the net of capital gains/losses, pension income (exclusive of Social Security), and any annuity or IRA distributions. To this total, add one-half of the person's annual Social Security benefit. If the sum of these is greater than $34,000 for a single taxpayer or $44,000 for a married couple, you fail the provisional income test and your Social Security benefit is now taxed at the 85% threshold. This increase has caused many retirees to pay much more in taxes over the last decade. Many have done nothing to counter the increase; they just pay more federal income tax.

Avoid the mistake

Review Line 8a and line 9a (interest and dividends) of your most recent tax return. For many retirees, this number is large because of their stockpiles of cash in savings accounts, certificates of deposit, or treasuries. For others it has become large due to investing in dividend producing investments since the financial crisis of 2008. The interest and dividends these funds produce may be causing you to fail the provisional income test. This may be the root cause of the 85 percent Social Security threshold!

Consider a shift to tax-efficient or tax-deferred investments to reduce Line 8a or 9a on the tax return to a level where you would pass the provisional income test and enjoy the Social Security benefit without counting it as a taxable event. This is what you expected when you enrolled in the system in the first place.

There are several techniques to properly eliminate or reduce the implications of this tax problem. We will illustrate just one example below for ease of learning:

Using a tax-deferred annuity to solve the problem is one method. In addition to an annuity, shifting assets to "tax efficient" planning also works well to reduce the exposure to the added tax. We will illustrate this with an example of a couple that is currently failing the provisional income test:

Mr. and Mrs. John Client have been enjoying their retirement years. Their total household income is $55,000, and they have an adjusted gross income of $52,000. Not all Social Security benefits are taxable, as shown below.

Wages	$ 0
Interest/Div (line 8a &9a	$20,000
Pension	$15,000
Social Security (line 20a)	$20,000

As described earlier, determining how much of Social Security is taxable is a two-part process. First, determine the household income exclusive of Social Security benefits paid.

Interest/Div (line 8a& 9a)	$20,000
Pension	$15,000
Household income	$35,000

Second, add the household income and one-half the annual Social Security benefit.

Household income	$35,000
One-half annual Social Security benefit	$10,000
	$45,000

The sum of $45,000 is greater than the top of the provisional income threshold of $44,000. As a result, this couple is taxed on 85 percent of their $20,000 Social Security benefit, increasing their taxable earnings by $6,850.

How to return Social Security back to TAX FREE status:

Mr. and Mrs. Client decide to shift most of their bank cash (which they don't plan to use but like to keep safe) into a fixed annuity. The interest is not taxable unless withdrawn. The results:

Wages	$ 0
Interest/Div (line 8a&9a)	$ 3,000
Pension	$15,000
Social Security	$20,000

First, determine the household income exclusive of Social Security benefits paid. Next, add one-half of the annual Social Security benefit.

Household income	$18,000
One-half Social Security benefit	$10,000
	$28,000

This $28,000 is less than the bottom provisional income test of $32,000. As a result, the clients are taxed on NONE of their Social Security benefit. This decreases their taxable earnings by nearly $7,000. This has been accomplished simply by shifting the manner in which they allocate their savings.

Many retirees make the mistake of focusing on estate taxes and forget about using techniques that prevent the confiscation of wealth via income taxation. The income tax consequences of your actions or inactions can make a world of difference for you and your family. Spend some time reviewing your tax returns and consider seeking advice to determine what planning opportunities would be best suited for your goals and objectives.

Chapter 18
Case Studies

Congratulations for having made it to the end of the book! Even though this is just an introductory book, we believe you can see how complex the fields of Estate Planning and Medicaid Planning are, and how expert advice is needed to use these laws effectively. We thought it would be helpful if we were to close the book with a few case studies. These are all real-life examples of situations that we have seen in our practice:

Case Study No. 1
Spouse in Nursing Home, No Planning Has Been Done
Joe and Nina have been married for fifty years, and have two middle-aged children. Here are their assets:

House	$300,000
Joint savings	$150,000
Joe IRA	$100,000
Nina IRA	$100,000

In addition, Joe is a veteran. He has a VA term life insurance policy of $20,000.

In this situation, for Medicaid purposes, the house is not a countable asset, and neither is the life insurance, since it is a term policy with no cash value. Everything else is a countable asset. The countable assets total $350,000. Nina goes into a nursing home. Joe can keep the house and $120,900 worth of cash. The rest, $229,100 has to be spent down. They spend down the money and Nina goes on Medicaid. Joe is left with the house and $120,900.

Joe and Nina have old wills that they did many years ago. Additionally, Nina is the beneficiary on Joe's remaining IRA funds. When Nina went into the nursing home, Joe did not remove Nina's name from the deed; nor did he change any of his estate planning documents. Joe gets sick and dies before Nina. Because Joe never changed his documents, Nina will inherit the $300,000 house and Joe's $120,900, *i.e.*, assets worth $420,900. She will immediately become ineligible for Medicaid, and she will need to spend down those assets on her care. If Nina lives long enough, the children could wind up with nothing. Had Joe simply removed Nina's name from the deed, done a simple trust and changed his IRA beneficiary designation, the assets would have gone to the children, and not Nina. Her care would have remained exactly the same, and the inheritance would not have been lost.

Case Study No. 2
Married Couple, No Durable Power of Attorney, Husband has Significant IRA

Jerry and Charlotte have been married for many years. Jerry was the sole breadwinner. He worked for a successful company and he has an IRA worth approximately $1 million.

He and Charlotte have a lovely home in an upscale neighborhood. The homeowner's association dues are $500 a month and property taxes are $1,000 a month. Heating and air conditioning costs average $400 a month. Maintenance of the pool averages $150 per month. Because Charlotte never worked outside the home, her Social Security benefits are minimal. Jerry is older than Charlotte, and he knows that, statistically, men usually die before women. He is comforted to know, however, that his IRA will be more than enough for Charlotte to live in their nice home, as well as provide her with a comfortable lifestyle. The couple has a will, and they signed medical powers of attorney at the hospital, but they never signed durable financial powers of attorney.

Jerry suffers a stroke, and needs permanent nursing home care. Charlotte knows that she can keep the house and $120,900. Because all of the money is in an IRA, Charlotte knows that the IRA will need to be cashed in, and that the income tax will be approximately $350,000. She does not have a particular problem with this, however, as she knows that eventually the taxes would need to be paid anyway, and the remaining funds, $650,000 are far more than sufficient to meet her needs.

Charlotte has read this book, and now knows that after subtracting $120,900 from the $650,000 left after taxes, she would have $529,100, and that she could make Jerry eligible for Medicaid if she used that money to purchase an irrevocable, non-assignable immediate annuity. Therefore, she is not worried about her financial future.

Charlotte contacts the company which manages Jerry's IRA to begin the cash-in process. The representative asks for a copy of Jerry's power of attorney. Here Charlotte hits a brick wall: Jerry has never signed a power of attorney. Therefore, Charlotte has no legal right to represent Jerry, and the company holding the IRA will not talk to her any further. Charlotte is in a panic.

Charlotte contacts an Elder Law Attorney, and learns that she will need to apply to the probate court to become Jerry's guardian. Not having any choice, Charlotte does this and the guardianship is approved. Now that she is Jerry's legal representative, the IRA custodian is authorized to speak with her, and follow her instructions to liquidate the account. Unfortunately Charlotte is unable to use the money to purchase an annuity without permission of the probate court. Therefore, she spends money to hire an attorney, who pleads her case to the court. However, she is not yet in financial distress, and other than sheltering money from the nursing home, there is no legal reason for the probate judge to grant her request to purchase the annuity. Therefore, her request is denied.

Crestfallen, Charlotte has no choice but to use the $529,100 to pay the nursing home. After all of this money is gone, all she has left is $120,900 and Jerry goes on Medicaid. Recall that Charlotte and Jerry have a nice house with expensive upkeep costs. Charlotte can no longer afford to keep this house. She needs to sell it and move. She is devastated, as all of the life plans she and Jerry made have been dashed.

Case Study No. 3
Same Couple, But with a Power of Attorney

Now let's stick with the same example, but change the facts a bit. In this new example, Jerry has signed a Durable

Power of Attorney which gives Charlotte the right to manage his IRA. Charlotte contacts the IRA custodian, and sends them a copy of the Power of Attorney. She instructs them to liquidate the IRA and withhold income tax. Charlotte now has a check for $530,000.

She puts $120,900 in the bank, and uses the rest of the money to purchase a five-year immediate annuity contract. The annuity will pay her approximately $8,900 a month for the next five years. She applies for Medicaid for Jerry, and the application is approved. Charlotte can keep the house and the $120,900. Her monthly living expenses, including taxes, home upkeep, food, insurance, etc. are approximately $3,900. Out of the $8,900 a month the annuity pays her, she spends $3,900 on her expenses, and puts the rest of the money, $5,000, in the bank. At the end of the five years, she has the $120,900 she started out with, plus $300,000 (from the $5,000 net monthly annuity payments over 60 months), for a total of $420,900. Although it is less than the $1 million she started with, she still has her nice house, plus enough money for financial security and dignity for the rest of her life. All in all, this is a far prettier picture than Case Study No. 2.

Case Study No. 4
Single Person, Lake House in Medicaid Trust

Now, let's look at an unmarried person. George is a widower with two children. He has about $150,000 in combined savings and IRAs, a modest house in the city, and a lakefront cottage on Governor's Island in Lake Winnipesaukee. George has worked his whole life as a janitor. There is no way he could have afforded the Winnipesaukee property on his salary. However, George's parents bought this property in 1942 for $5,000. George inherited it when they died and it is now worth well over $1 million. Although paying the property taxes is a struggle, George loves to live at the cottage in the summer, and, needless to say, his children and grandchildren love it as well. George doesn't mind using his money and the equity in his city house to pay for a nursing home should he need one, but protecting the lake property is supremely important to him.

Some years ago, George visited with an Elder Law Attorney, and he put the lake house into a Medicaid trust. George and his family have continued to use the cottage as normal over the years, and the fact that the title is in a trust has had no noticeable impact on his life. Unfortunately, however, George develops Alzheimer Disease. His condition worsens, and his children have no choice but to place him in a nursing home.

The nursing home costs $11,000 per month. George's children use the $150,000 savings George has, and, when that runs out, they sell his city house and use the proceeds for the nursing home for about two years. This is all right with them, because George had said that he wanted those assets to pay for his care, if necessary. However, George wanted the lake house protected. Fortunately, George had the foresight to put the lake house into the Medicaid Trust. George's children apply for Medicaid, which is approved, and the lake cottage is protected. When George dies, his trust terminates, and the children inherit the cottage. George has paid his own way at the nursing home for a few years, and has passed an important legacy to his family.

Case Study No. 5
Married Couple, Massachusetts, Estate Tax

Dana and Barbara live in North Andover, Massachusetts. They are in their eighties, and have lived in the same house since 1962. When they bought the house, it cost them what was then the princely sum of $45,000. At the time, they actually thought that they overpaid, but they really loved the house, and the town was safe and had excellent schools. It was easy commuting distance to Dana's job in Lawrence. Due to the run-up in Massachusetts real estate prices, in addition to the fact that there is a premium for living in a sought-after town, their house has appreciated to $645,000. Whenever they get their tax bill showing the assessment, they can't believe it. They both worked for the phone company, and got excellent benefits. Dana has an IRA of $250,000 and Barbara has an IRA of $250,000. In addition, Dana was a great believer in corporate bonds, and he now has bonds worth $175,000. Their children added up all of these assets, and let Dana and Barbara know that they have an estate of over $1.3 million. Even though they have done the math themselves, they live a very simple lifestyle, and are not quite convinced that they are "millionaires."

Dana and Barbara have simple wills, leaving all of the assets to the other spouse. Dana dies, and Barbara inherits it all. She then dies a few years later. Because her estate is worth $1.3 million, at her death there is a tax due the Commonwealth of about $52,000.

Now let's change the facts. Instead of having simple wills, Dana and Barbara each sign a separate Revocable Trust. A half interest in the house and the bonds was put into each trust. Because the law prohibits trusts from owning retirement plans, the IRAs had to remain in their personal names. Thus, their estate was as follows:

Dana Trust Half of House	322,500
Dana Trust Half of Corporate Bonds	87,500
Dana IRA	250,000
Total Estate, Dana	660,000
Barbara Trust Half of House	322,500
Barbara Trust Half of Corporate Bonds	87,500
Barbara IRA	250,000
Total Estate, Dana	660,000

Now look what happens when each party dies. At Dana's death, no tax return needs to be filed, as his estate is under $1 million. His half of the house and bonds goes into the family trust which is a part of his revocable trust. Barbara can draw on this trust if she needs to, but ownership of the trust is not in her estate. Barbara inherits Dana's $250,000 IRA.

At Barbara's death, her estate includes her half of the house and bonds, her IRA and Dana's IRA, for a total of $910,000. Her total estate is under $1 million, so no estate tax return is filed and no estate tax is due. By preparing and funding the two trusts during their life, they have saved their children approximately $52,000 in estate taxes.

Chapter 19
Where Do I Go From Here?

If the readers of this book are like most of our clients, they are individuals who have worked a lifetime building up a nest egg. They have worked hard, paid their mortgage and taxes, provided for their families, and put money aside. Rather than complain or give up when life put obstacles in their path, they kept on doing what they were taught as children: be diligent and work hard.

This generation has historically been the most successful in the ability to save and invest money. However, as all older adults know, there is a sure-fire way to lose most, if not all, of a lifetime of savings quickly: to go into a nursing home long-term. Our clients are people who believe in paying their own way. Accepting a "handout" from anyone goes against every bone in their body. That being said, however, our clients also know that there is something very wrong in our society when they are forced to pay $11,000 or $12,000 a month to a nursing facility. There is something very wrong when the healthy spouse is forced to live in poverty, or near poverty. There is something very wrong when an application for Medicaid takes five or six months. There is something very wrong when going through the

Medicaid application process makes older adults feel drained and exhausted. It is a sad fact that becoming disabled in our country is more expensive than dying, and that leaving a modest inheritance to your spouse, children or other loved ones is something that the Medicaid laws have made very difficult.

We hope that you have found this book helpful. The issue of long-term care planning is very complex, and no one plan fits every situation. We have designed this book to help you better understand the devastating financial consequences a long-term nursing home stay can have on you and your loved ones, and the types of strategies we use to help our clients avoid financial devastation.

Many readers of this book will already have started their estate plans, in the sense that they have put at least a will in place. However, most people have not put in place a plan for what would happen should they need a long-term nursing home stay. As you read this final chapter, take a moment and ask yourself whether you have a strategy for coping with a long-term nursing home stay. Have your legal and financial advisors even discussed this with you? We so often hear that the answer is "no."

So, congratulations on taking the first big step by reading this book and becoming more informed. The next step should be to transform your knowledge into action. If you would like to discuss in more detail how the authors of this book may help you and your family protect your lifetime of savings, we would be pleased to speak with you. Beasley & Ferber may be reached at 1-800-370-5010 and Affinity Investment Group may be reached at 1-877-858-8156.

Appendix

Glossary

Advance Directive

A document used in New Hampshire which contains a power of attorney for health care and a living will.

Annuity

There are many types of annuities, but for purposes of this book, an annuity is a financial device which converts assets into income, thereby protecting the funds from nursing home spenddown.

Attorney-in-Fact

Also known as an "Agent,", this is a person who is empowered by a Durable Power of Attorney to manage finances or business.

Caretaker Child

An adult child who provides care to his or her parent, such that the parent is kept out of a nursing home for two years. The parent's house might be able to be transferred to the Caretaker Child if certain legal requirement are met.

Community Spouse

The spouse of a nursing home resident.

Conservator

In Massachusetts, a court-appointed person who manages the finances or health care of an incapacitated person.

Durable Power of Attorney

A document which names an Agent, also known as an Attorney-in-Fact. This person takes care of your business and financial affairs if you become incompetent or incapacitated.

Estate Tax

A tax on an inheritance. The federal exemption is $5.49 million and the Massachusetts exemption is $1 million.

Executor

In New Hampshire, the person who administers the estate of someone who has died.

Fair Hearing

An appeal of an adverse decision from the Medicaid agency.

Fiduciary

Someone who manages the money or property belonging to another, such as an Attorney-in-Fact or executor.

Guardian over the Estate

In New Hampshire, a court-appointed person who manages the finances or business affairs of someone who is incompetent.

Guardian over the Person

In New Hampshire, a court-appointed person who manages the health care decisions of someone who is incompetent.

Health Care Proxy

In Massachusetts, a document which serves as a power of attorney for health care matters.

HIPAA

Stands for Health Insurance Portability and Accountability Act. This is the medical privacy law.

Incompetent

A person who is incapacitated to the extent that he or she cannot make legal, financial or medical judgments.

Individual Retirement Account (IRA)

A retirement account that grows on a tax deferred basis until age 70.5, when required distributions must commence.

Inflation Rider

An amendment to a long-term care insurance policy which states that the benefit increases each year.

Institutionalized Spouse

A nursing home resident who is married.

Life Estate

A term inserted into a deed by which the grantor is allowed to remain living in the property.

Living Will

A document which states that if you are terminally ill with no hope of recovery, you do not wish to receive extraordinary measures or life support.

Living Trust

See entry for Revocable Trust.

Lookback Period

The five-year period prior to a Medicaid application during which the state Medicaid agency reviews the assets of a Medicaid applicant.

Long-Term Care Insurance

A type of health insurance policy which will cover nursing home and/or home health care costs.

Medicaid

The joint federal & state program which pays nursing home and other health costs for persons with a minimal level of assets.

Medicaid Trust

An irrevocable trust which is designed to protect real estate or financial assets from nursing home spend-down.

Medicaid Planning

A process by which assets are sheltered, or protected, so that someone can qualify for Medicaid.

Medicare

Basic health insurance for people over age 65. Often confused with Medicaid, but the two are completely different.

Net Unrealized Appreciation (NUA)

NUA occurs when an employer-sponsored retirement plan allows the employee to purchase employer securities as part of the plan. The IRS treats these securities than it treats other assets when an employee retires. When the employee rolls over his retirement plan to an IRA, he/she can withdraw & sell the employer securities and pay income tax based on the cost basis and capital gains tax on the gain. The cash, mutual funds, or other investment accounts will roll over to the IRA and are not taxed until withdrawn.

Penalty Period

A period of time during which someone is ineligible for Medicaid, due to having made gifts within the five year period preceding a Medicaid application.

Personal Representative

In Massachusetts, the person who manages the estate of someone who has died.

Protected person

In Massachusetts, an incapacitated person who is the subject of conservatorship.

Provisional income

The sum of a person's wages if still employed, interest, dividends, the net of capital gains/losses, pension income (exclusive of Social Security), and any annuity or IRA distributions. The result determines amount of taxable Social Security benefits.

Revocable Trust

Also known as a Living Trust, a document which serves as a substitute for a will, and avoids probate proceedings after someone has died.

Special Power of Appointment

A term inserted into an irrevocable trust or deed which allows changes to the beneficiaries or the people to whom the property was deeded.

Spenddown

The process of depleting assets in order to meet eligibility for Medicaid.

Spousal Impoverishment Law

A law which states that a spouse of someone in a nursing home is allowed to keep a specified minimal amount of money.

Summary Administration:

A probate proceeding in New Hampshire in which a formal accounting is not required.

Testator

A person who signs a will.

Voluntary Administration:

A probate procedure in Massachusetts for certain small estates.

Waiver of Administration

A simplified probate proceeding in New Hampshire for certain estates.

Ward

In New Hampshire, an incapacitated person who is the subject of a guardianship